Submit or Else
&
Lessons from yester-women's lives

- Philile Twala Mwangi –

I0142952

eFeM Creations CC

Copyrights

Copyright © 2014 *eFeM Creations CC*.
All rights reserved.

Copyright notice: No part of this publication may be reproduced or transmitted in any form or by any means, or stored in any retrieval system of any nature without the prior written permission of the copyright holder. The copyright holder assumes no liability for errors or omissions.

ISBN Number: 978-0-620-53938-8

Book *Published* and *Distributed* by: *eFeM Creations C.C.*

e-Mail: efem.creations@gmail.com

Book Cover Design By:

Nazia Bacus

Book Illustrations Done By:

Dane Knudsen

Book Editing & Layout Design By:

Festus M. Mwangi

Dedication

To all women

ACKNOWLEDGEMENTS

First and foremost, I would like to register my utmost gratitude to the Almighty God; without His divine inspiration, guidance and mysterious revelations, this book would not have come to be. Glory and honour be unto Him, Always...!

In addition, I feel greatly indebted to my unexpected silent and verbally represented critics; you have served as my passive proof of the need, and motivation in the compilation of this book.

Special thanks also go to my mom and sister Sebbie, the two women who have actively and intimately been in my life the longest; your unconditional love and support in diverse ways is most appreciated.

To my clients as a beauty therapist, thanks to you all for opening up, sharing and confiding in me. Our conversations led me to seeing the dire need for alleviation of the society's ignorance and misconception associated with *Submission*.

To my dear soul-mate and loving husband, this book would not have taken the shape it has without your selfless and tireless editing. It must have been such a piece of work tying-up the bits and scraps together. Your serving as my sounding board for the content in its raw form has been invaluable. Your feedback and constructive reflection of my submissiveness to you has been phenomenal in pointing me towards becoming a better person, woman, mother, wife, and writer.

My utmost gratitude also goes to my children; Sandiso, Emma, Henry, and Milani. You have tested me in almost every possible way one can think of. You have also served as a good training ground for exercising kindness and patience as part of my ability to give and receive love. Besides Biblical teachings, you have instilled in me an ever growing sense and drive to control and restrain myself from judging others.

Throughout the time-span of writing this book, I have had to feed on God's *Word* and have significantly grown up from the 'child' I was. This would not have been possible without the resourceful networks like TBN and Rhema. I want to particularly acknowledge my appreciation for sermons from my local parish priest, and the numerous wonderful Pastors on the television networks and the Trans-World Radio Station; you have served me with real spiritual food for this incredible journey.

Lastly, and not in any way the least, I would like to thank the proof readers, graphic designers, and every other person who has in any way contributed to the publication of this Book; your positive input is most appreciated and most probably the ounce that tipped the scale. May all your particular contributions bear fruits towards bringing Glory and honour to the Almighty Living God.

Be blessed.

Pypie.

Table of Content

Introduction

$\mathcal{T}$his book mainly focuses on how women, married and single women alike, can learn about submission. However, great emphasis is on the vitality of submission in marriage. We explore the lives of women of the Bible who have gone before us in order to learn from their lives about submission in its different forms. We especially learn that it all starts by *submitting* to God, who then gives us the strength and wisdom to *submit* to our earthly authorities.

We learn from some Biblical women who took God out of the equation of their lives and suffered the consequences of their actions. We also realize that even though their life stories are based on a different life time from ours, life itself is still the same today; we have certainly improved in terms of technology but everything else is just the same. As such, many real-life lessons can be drawn from them.

Similarly we learn from another set of women of the Bible who clearly exemplify the joy, fruits and / or rewards that come with full submission. Parallel to the lives of women who failed to *submit,* we see submission reverberating as a natural law, just like the commonly known laws of nature such as the universal gravitational law, law of attraction, and the law of forces (action versus reaction). All in all, we get to see the superseding dominion of God's grace in both contexts of successful and failed submission.

I hope that as women we can learn from the lives of our fore-mothers and apply it in our own current life. This would give us a better life on this earth and the lessons learnt can be passed on to our children. I trust that, with God's divine revelation and Grace, everyone of us can fathom the full dimensions of the marriage covenant. I pray that every woman gets to meaningfully identify with Ruth when she said to Naomi, her mother in law:

"Don't ask me to leave you! Let me go with you. Wherever you go, I will go; wherever you live, I will live. Your people will be my people, and your God will be my God. Wherever you die, I will die, and that is where I will be buried. May the LORD's worst punishment come upon me if I let anything but death separate me from you!"

- Ruth 1: 16-17 [GNT] -

Submit or Else

Submit or Else

*C*ontroversial as the topic of *submission* is, I will trying to desensitize it and make it more of a reality than a war-cry, especially to women. I seek to highlight the virtuous aspects of it, as opposed to the conventionally imminent *demon* it is purported or perceived to be, and in other instances the *evil* or *negative vibe* that it is associated with.

It is very important for us to bear in mind that God is always on our side; He is not out to punish us after we have failed to *submit* [...'sinned' or 'missed the mark' as some people would like to view it...] – No-o-o...! - He wants us to *submit* to Him because He loves us so dearly. As you will see, our submission to Him is for our own good.

Some people have the mentality that once they have failed to *submit*, then God will surely stop loving them. However, that is not the case and nothing could be as far from the truth; [1]God is rich in His grace and mercy. [2]His love for us is unconditional and never fails. Nevertheless, what happens as a result of failed submission is that sin catches up with us and brings along stacks

---

[1] Ephesians 1:7 & Ephesians 2:4

[2] Romans 5:8 ; Ephesians 3:16-19; Psalms 36:5-7;Isaiah 49:15-16; Zephaniah 3:17; Ephesians 2:4-5; Psalm 48:9; Jeremiah 31:3; Psalm 136:26; Lamentations 3:22 – 25; 1 John 4:9-10; John 3:16-17; Titus 3: 4-5; 1 John 3:1; Romans 8: 35-39; 1 John 4:16; Psalm 52:8; John 13:1

of misfortunes in our lives. Submission operates just in the same way as what *Sir Isaac Newton* found out and defined as a Law of Forces - *for every action there is a reaction*; whether you choose to *submit* or not, there will certainly be a reaction to your choice of action. That is why the [3]Bible advises us to follow the action of *submitting* because it triggers positive reactions.

In that respect, submission may be seen in the light similar to that of the other acclaimed universal laws of nature, such as the law of attraction, the law of gravity and the like: always surpassing time, always accurate, always true, always grossly universal, and always prevailing regardless of whether one is aware of their existence or not...!

What does it mean to *submit*?

To [4]*submit*, in a broad sense and in simplest terms, means to *obey*. The two terms go hand in hand and they are hereby contextually meant to be perceived as being mutually inclusive. When you *submit* to anyone, be it God, your husband, King or anyone else, it means that you *obey* that person. For the purposes only of delivering the message of *Submission* in this Book, 'to *obey*' is conceived to mean 'to *respect* and / or

---

[3] Isaiah 3:10
[4] Thesaurus: English (UK).

honour', as opposed to heeding to some stipulated rules.

In the [5]Bible, *submission* refers to an attitude of obedience, support, respect, honour and co-operation.

From a [6]text transcript on the message preached on christian *submission* at Elijah Ministries, the preacher invites us to consider a military leader who doesn't have the support and co-operation of his troop. Surely as the preacher puts it, such a leader is on a hiding second to none...!

According to [7]Fritz Rienecker and Cleon Rogers, the word *submission* translates from the Greek word *hupotasso*, which is a cognate of the preposition *hupo*, meaning "under" and the stem *tasso*, meaning "to arrange." In the first century, this word was used as a military term as well as a description of the behaviour of a servant to his master.

Other definitions are available in numerous other resources like the dictionary, encyclopaedia and free internet sources like the *Wikipedia*. The general impression is that submission extends to include divine hierarchy. It is therefore not just for

[5] Psalm 111: 10; Mark 12: 30; John 14: 5; 1 Samuel 15: 23; Hebrews 13:17; 1 Peter 2: 13-15; Philippians 2:5-11; Ephesians 4: 17-24

[6] Elijah Ministries. [Online]. *Christian submission.* Available at: http://africanaquatics.co.za/_christian/_articles/submission.htm. (Accessed 29 Oct. 2011)

[7] Fritz Rienecker, and Cleon Rogers. *Linguistic Key to the Greek New Testament,* (pg.538), Zondervan; English Edition (April 1982)

women but also for all men and children as well. Regardless of the various interpretations, synonyms, and contextual applications of the word *Submit*, this book is a concerted call upon one and all to **first** submit to the Lord our God, the ultimate authority.

As you may already know, God is the Creator and Ruler of the world that we live in (*Genesis 1 & 2*). Nevertheless, this truth has been twisted by the devil to the effect of it seeming like the world is *"ruled"* by the devil himself in reality *(Ephesians 2:2)*. Perhaps you should also know at this point that the devil is a master of counterfeits (…*piracy* and other forms of infringement of intellectual property rights…). He has his pirated version of God's *Submission* master-piece; we may generally refer to it as the *Worldly-submission*. It will be explored further shortly after understanding the divine hierarchy of submission.

In general, and for the objective of this book, submission has largely been categorized into three levels: Submission to God, submission in marriage, and worldly submission.

(1) Submission to God

It is God first that we must *submit* to before we can even consider trying to *submit* to other people. All our submission needs to be aligned with God's *Word*. It is critical that we obey God, which means that we follow His ways. By so doing He will enable us to *submit* to the authority He has placed in our lives and He will give us the wisdom to do so.

[8]Jesus said to His disciples: "If you love me, you will obey my commandments." Paraphrasing this statement we can say: "If you love me, you will *submit* to my commandments". The first question that we should ask ourselves then is what Jesus' commandments are. It is notably very clear that He is not referring to the 10 commandments, yet He was the only man ever on this planet who ever fulfilled those 10 commandments to the letter.

Jesus' commandments to us

1. [9]"...Love the Lord your God with all your heart, with all your soul, and with all your mind."

This is the greatest and most important commandment.

2. [10]"Love your neighbour as you love yourself."

This is the second most important commandment.

Elsewhere in the Gospel of John, this second commandment is written as:

---

[8] John 14:15
[9] Mathew 22:37
[10] Mathew 22:39

"Love one another. As I have loved you, so you must love one another." - John 14:34.

From what Jesus said, I see a strong relationship between LOVE and SUBMISION, and as further reinforced by *Honour* and *Obedience*.

How?

Since to *submit* also means to obey and honour, therefore Jesus was similarly saying that "if you love me you will obey me, you will honour me, you will *submit* to me." In other words, by not honouring Him, by not obeying Him and by not *submitting* to Him, it would implicitly mean that we do not love Him.

So, that is why Jesus commands us to love God above all things and to love our neighbour as we love ourselves. This is because He knew that it will be impossible for us to *submit* to God and to one another if we do not operate in love. If love is the key to submission, then what does it mean to love?

The apostle Paul gave a good description of what it really means to love; as you read, it becomes very clear why God is Love:

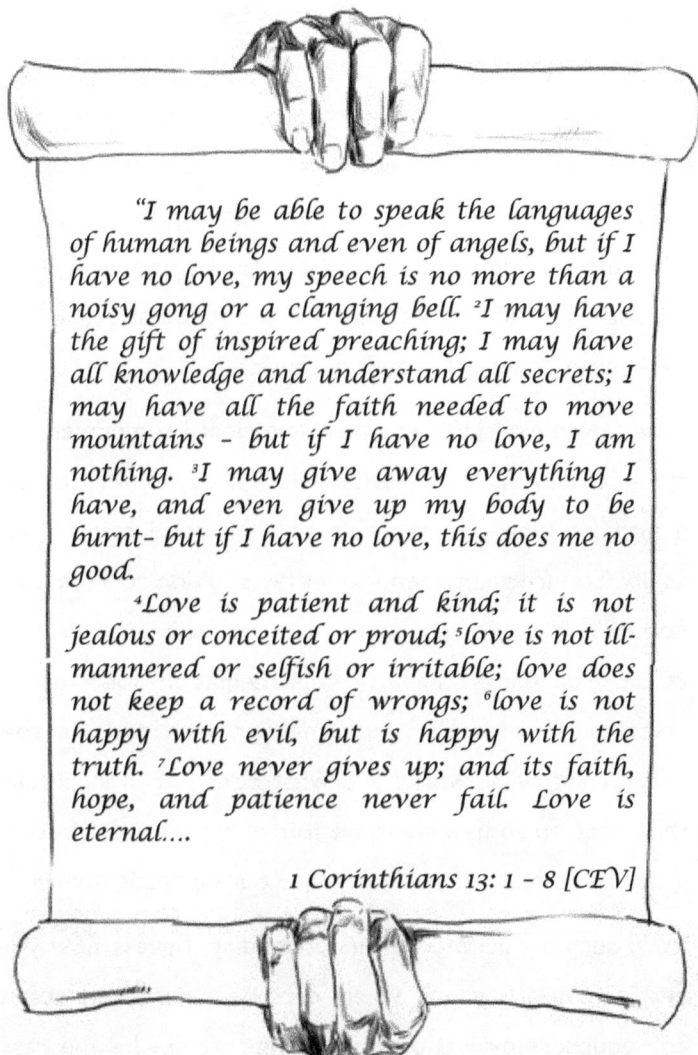

"I may be able to speak the languages of human beings and even of angels, but if I have no love, my speech is no more than a noisy gong or a clanging bell. ²I may have the gift of inspired preaching; I may have all knowledge and understand all secrets; I may have all the faith needed to move mountains - but if I have no love, I am nothing. ³I may give away everything I have, and even give up my body to be burnt- but if I have no love, this does me no good.

⁴Love is patient and kind; it is not jealous or conceited or proud; ⁵love is not ill-mannered or selfish or irritable; love does not keep a record of wrongs; ⁶love is not happy with evil, but is happy with the truth. ⁷Love never gives up; and its faith, hope, and patience never fail. Love is eternal....

1 Corinthians 13: 1 - 8 [CEV]

This kind of love is eminently the real deal; if only we can all be possessed by it...!

In my opinion, the toughest parts of Love is "*Kind* and *patient* " - I'm still struggling with being kind and patient especially with my children when they sometimes decide to just do the opposite of what I tell them to do. The words that come out of my mouth during such episodes are nothing close to being kind. Sometimes I even feel like I should give myself a hiding or ground myself in an effort to erase the guilt that befalls me after such mean bouts of uncouth outbursts.

I can't even explain to you how impatient I sometimes get with my *hubby*; for instance, I pride myself in having what people call a high intuition - I prefer to call it a good spiritual hearing ability. So I frequently tend to let my intuition guide me. On the contrary, it strikes me across like he believes in proving the efficacy of things through implementation followed by an assessment ... it's like experimenting with real life towards determining what works and what does not. I am inclined to think that, to some extent, his flair of being a researcher in the scientific domain has spilt over into our domestic domain.

With such a reference of understanding, I guess now you can imagine what happens when decision-making and results or consequences evaluation time comes; Yeap...! - the resultant off-the-cuff fire-works-propelled darts from me like ... 'I told you so!', 'you <u>never</u> listen to me!', 'You <u>always</u> do this!' and so forth. And hey, kindly keep this between me and you - my own family has been a really good practicing ground for my love to be "kind and patient."

On another footing, love does not keep a record of wrongs! — that is a tough one for almost everyone, and I can even *taste a sword* on that. As for me, the tendency to refer to the past instances is almost inevitable. It is like that itchy feeling on your elbow that will just hang on and not go away however hard you stump your foot on the ground...!

Of course I do have forgiveness in my heart; the problem is forgetting. Notice the underlined *never* and *always* in my variety of ammunitions. It's like they have been deeply engraved into my sub-conscious mind. Just like I alluded to, I am very sure that I am not walking alone on this tight rope between forgiving and forgetting. And I bet you also like Roy Acuff's song, hey? - *I'll Forgive You but I Can't Forget...*

It is our deliberate failure to delete off in our memories the wrongs done unto us that has partly led to the so many unhappy marriages, escalating divorce rates, and the resultant hike in the number of children from broken homes. Most people say 'enough is enough!' when filing for a divorce. The pertinent question is: enough of what? It appears to me like that disposition directly alludes to the count of their partner's offences dating as far back as they know when, till the snapping point of finally deciding to give up. I am of the view that, if we could all just work hard on perfecting this part of our love, then the rate of divorce would drop drastically. This is based on the premise that each day would be started on a clean page of no memory of your partner ever hurting your feelings. It may be a daunting challenge, but I think it still is a jar worth fighting for before the milk gets sour...!

Do you realize that the moment we operate in love in our lives, it means we are functioning under God's guidance? The very same love that will make it easy for us to *submit* is God Himself, which means that we will be having God's Spirit in us if we are operating in love. This means that before we can even imagine of ourselves being able to *submit* to God, our husband, and parents. We first have to operate under the sedation of love.

Remember - [11]God is Love. This basically means that we will only be able to properly *submit* if we allow God to make our hearts His home. This implicitly means that if we fail to *submit* to either God, our parents, husbands and children, then we do

[11] 1 John 4:8

not love them, and that lack of love (...lack of God's Spirit), makes it impossible to *submit*.

Put in another way, if you keep doing things that are not aligned properly with God's *Word*, we are simply keeping on dishonouring and disobeying God's *Word*. This indirectly means that we dishonour God and love the devil. As we already know, it is not possible to drive two cars at the same time. You do hereby realize that there are no *in-betweeners* in this context, i.e. we are either for God or for the devil. And hey, just in case we insist on being in the middle, then we automatically fall on the devil's side by default. Please take note here that this relativity does not in any way imply that God and the Devil are *equally* opposing sides; God is supreme...!

Therefore, we will only be able to *submit* to God and our husbands if we love God. No matter how they behave, let us strive to unconditionally love our husbands, children, and parents. Only then will *submitting* to them become *easier* (...if not *easy*). Kindly remember that this is not just for women but for *all* mankind; the call is to first *submit* to the Lord our God.

Unfortunately over the years, evil-possessed men have abused their authority over women, making the call of submission to be associated with abuse, yet that is not how it is like. Let us bear in mind that all the people who have abused 'submission' at some point have done so on their own account at the expense of following God's *Word*. This includes even church leaders, who would then misquote God's *Word* to make it fit with their wrong doings. A lot of abuse and forceful controlling has been inflicted on, or directed towards women in the name of 'submission'. Accordingly, it is no wonder why many women do not want anything to do with it anymore or unconsciously cock their guns at the mention of the word.

(2) Submission in marriage

Submission in marriage is one of the most important levels of submission. Going by the statistics of divorce rates, it looks like the devil figured out that part of the equation long ago because marriage as an institution has been under attack from the beginning of times.

The absence of submission in a marriage is a sure fuel for trouble.

Yet marriage is God's greatest plan and if messed up, it brings forth a chain reaction of destruction in the world.

Look at what is happening around the world; divorces are still prevalent in our society. Why do you think that is so? If marriage is not all that important to God, then why do you think it is so much under attack? Simple - the devil is behind the scenes ... and cameras too, hey? - He knows that the fruits of a healthy marriage equate to a fulfilling life and that is why he is preoccupied with a mission to destroying this divine institution.

Submission in marriage primarily emanates from the wife as an action displayed from <u>her free will</u>. Therefore it is not the husband's duty to force her into submission, by beating her up, 'cold war', or verbally abusing her in the name of 'teaching her to *submit*'. Nowhere in the Bible is it written that men need or have to do this. Instead, the Bible says:

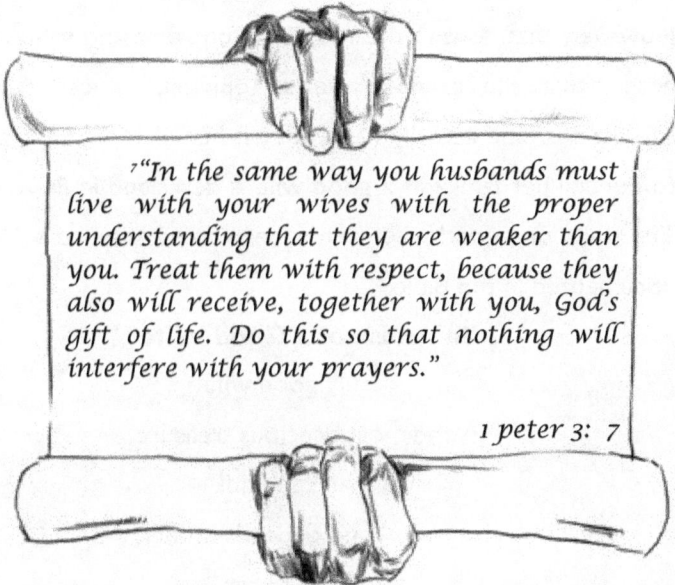

> ⁷*"In the same way you husbands must live with your wives with the proper understanding that they are weaker than you. Treat them with respect, because they also will receive, together with you, God's gift of life. Do this so that nothing will interfere with your prayers."*
>
> *1 peter 3: 7*

So, husbands are being advised in the scriptures to be gentle with their wives because women are physically *weaker* / fragile. A man who thinks his wife *submits* to him because he has taught her to by being harsh towards her is mistaken because that woman, or wife as is usually the case, will only acquiesce out of fear for her physical well-being. Love cannot thrive in fear.

Women have their role of supporting their respective husbands and should not act as the head of the house as it has become common practice today. It is written in the [12]Bible that women cannot have authority over men.

However, that doesn't mean that a woman has no value at her home, that she cannot have an opinion, or cannot make suggestions. She actually has a lot on her plate when it comes to nursing her family as a good wife is described in *Proverbs 31*. The traits of a good wife cannot be averred any better than as documented in the Bible:

In Praise of a Good Wife

A truly good wife

is the most precious treasure

a man can find!

Her husband depends on her,

and she never

---

[12] I Timothy 2:12; I Corinthians 14:34; Titus 2:5

lets him down.

She is good to him

every day of her life,

and with her own hands

she gladly makes clothes.

She is like a sailing ship

that brings food

from across the sea.

She gets up before daylight

to prepare food

for her family

and for her servants. She knows how to buy land

and how to plant a vineyard,

and she always works hard.

She knows when to buy or sell,

and she stays busy

until late at night.

She spins her own cloth,

and she helps the poor

and the needy.

Her family has warm clothing,

and so she doesn't worry

when it snows.

She does her own sewing,

and everything she wears

is beautiful.

Her husband is a well-known

and respected leader in the city.

She makes clothes to sell

to the shop owners.

She is strong and graceful, as well as cheerful

about the future.

Her words are sensible,

and her advice is thoughtful.

She takes good care

of her family

and is never lazy.

Her children praise her,

and with great pride

her husband says,

"There are many good women,

but you are the best!"

Charm can be deceiving,

and beauty fades away,

but a woman

who honours the LORD

deserves to be praised.

Show her respect--

praise her in public

for what she has done.

- [Proverbs 31: 10 - 31] -

Strive to be a good wife...!

A Christian woman should never reject the authority of her husband. Instead, she should serve him as she serves Christ; Christ is her *spiritual husband* and her husband is the *earthly husband*. Her husband represents Jesus to her as he is God's ordained authority over her in their marriage. If she chooses to reject his leadership, it all adds up to rejecting Jesus in her life, which means rejecting God.

Jesus said:

"Whoever listens to you listens to me. Whoever rejects you rejects me: and whoever rejects me rejects the one who sent me". — [Luke 10:16].

We learn that [13]when the Israelites rejected Prophet Samuel's leadership, God said that they did not just reject him (Samuel) but they rejected Him (God Himself). [14]A similar incident

[13] I Samuel 8
[14] Exodus 16:8

happened to Moses when the people of Israel were complaining against him and his brother Aaron. Moses said to them that their grumbling was actually against the LORD Himself. This just shows how significant God's-ordained authority is over our lives, which may be in the form of any leader and most importantly our husbands.

(3) Worldly Submission

In this world, submission is a very controversial topic that is avoided by many at all costs. It is perceived as a form of weakness in character. The world's idea of submission is for people to *submit* as little as possible. Therefore, numerous people are climbing the 'corporate ladder' in order to partly minimize the number of people to *submit* to. The higher one climbs up the ladder, the more successful they are considered to be.

The desire to climb the 'corporate ladder' doesn't stop until you probably get to be the one that everybody *submits* to. The goal of finally becoming the main *honcho* has become the pseudo-definition of success to the world.

This kind of belief is the one that put the devil into a hot soup. He too had dreams of climbing the ladder so high that he could be the one that everybody *submits* to. In the book of *Isaiah*, the devil is quoted to have said:

"...I will climb to heaven and place my throne above the highest star. I will sit there with the gods far away in the north. I will be above the clouds, just like God Most High"
- Isaiah 14:13-14 [CEV]

Therefore it's best for you to be guided by what God's *Word* says and not to follow worldly ideas. The tendency for people to choose worldly submission has even spread out to the church. Most Christians today, led by their selfish ambitions, will misquote some Bible verses in order to excuse their evil goal-driven intentions.

Hear me out here ... there is nothing wrong with having a high position at work, but what I'm addressing here is the wrong belief that sometimes drives people to yearn for promotion. If God is behind your promotion at work, well and good; you are blessed my dear and nothing can stop it. However, if you got it by your own means just so that you could feed your ego by feeling more important than everybody else, then that is a big problem.

The verse, [15]"And the Lord shall make you the head, and not

---

[15] Deuteronomy 28:13 [AMP]

the tail" is amongst the abused favourites. And YES, this verse is true - like our Father in heaven, we are to be leaders; leaders wherever God puts us. Even if you have a job that is regarded as "low" by the world's standards, God may have put you there to be your colleague's or boss' spiritual leader and will promote you to another job or assignment in due season.

In the battle for promotion, how come nobody seems to remember to quote Jesus when he said, [16]"Serve one another"? He explained that if you want to be a leader you must be ready serve others. He even demonstrated that by washing His disciples' feet.

- Supremacy of Divine Submission -

To easily understand the supremacy of Submission to God over all other forms of submission, let us relate with three instances involving Jesus and a family that He had a personal connection with; His three encounters with Mary and Martha.

(i) [17] *Mary sitting at Jesus' feet and upsetting Martha:*

Mary and Martha were the sisters of Jesus' dear friend. Jesus would go about teaching the *Word* of God in many towns accompanied by His disciples. There came a time when he went

[16] Galatians 5:13
[17] Luke 10:38-42

to the town where Mary and Martha lived. So He paid them a visit and Martha welcomed Him and got busy preparing a meal to serve Him. As Jesus had come with His disciples, that meant preparing a meal for at-least 13 people, and it must had been quite a task.

But as Martha was busy in the kitchen, cooking and serving their guests, her sister Mary left her working and sat at the feet of Jesus, listening to His teaching.

When Martha realized what her sister was doing, she was very upset and she went to Jesus saying:

"Lord, don't you care that my sister has left me to do all the work by myself? Tell her to come and help me!" - Luke 10:40 [GNT]

But Jesus answered her saying:

"Martha, Martha! You are worried [you are <u>careful</u> - KJV] about and troubled over so many things, but just one is needed. Mary has chosen the right thing, and it will not be taken away from her." - Luke 10:41-42 [GNT]

(ii) [18]*When their brother was raised to life:*

Lazarus fell ill and the two sisters sent a message to Jesus about their brother's illness. Regardless, he ended up dying because the Lord Jesus delayed going to them. And by the time Jesus got to their place, Lazarus had already been buried for 4 days. Upon His arrival, Martha went to meet Him and talked to Him. Then she went to Mary telling her that Jesus was calling her. So Mary went to meet Jesus at the same place where Martha had met Him. After they talked, Jesus then went on to raise their brother to life.

[18] John 11:38-53

(iii) [19]*When Mary anointed Jesus feet and Martha served:*
Sometime after Jesus had raised Lazarus to life, He paid them a visit and when he got there, Martha served Him and the disciples. To the contrary, Mary sat at Jesus feet and anointed them with an expensive perfume. One of the disciples {Judas} scolded her for using it, saying it was a waste as it could have been sold and the money used to support the poor. But it is common knowledge he only said this with an ulterior motives; he was the treasurer of Jesus' ministry and used to steal some of the money.

Lessons

Jesus introduced to mankind the idea of having a relationship with God instead of seeing Him as a distant super being. [20]When He taught us how to pray, saying "Our Father...", not only did He teach us that we are related to God but also that the relationship supersedes everything else. It is worthy noticing just how the prayer begins with the relationship and then everything else follows.

It was the Pharisees who wanted Jesus to be crucified; they were so religious that they even missed God when He was amongst them in flesh. On the other hand, Jesus' disciples were

[19] John 12:1-8
[20] Matthew 6:9-13 ; Luke 11:2-4

not religious but they had a relationship with Jesus. He was their teacher and friend. They learnt from Him so much that their lives changed forever.

We can show up in time every Sunday in church, put more money than everyone in the offering basket, sing louder than all, pray longer and with much deeper words **but** all these efforts would be a waste if we don't have a personal *relationship* with the Lord Jesus Christ. If we religiously do all that we do but miss out on the relationship that Jesus introduced us to, then we too may be like the Pharisees and be uncomfortable when the light of Jesus shines on us.

When we relate with Jesus, all He requires us to do is to **draw** from Him. [21]As He said that He is the living water, He therefore loves it when we see Him as that and just drink from Him, the thirst quenching water. He cherishes seeing us looking up to Him and not unto ourselves. On the contrary, religion will cause us to focus on ourselves. For instance, religion will teach us how we can serve the Lord just like Martha. It will drain us so much that we may even rebuke Jesus when we see fellow Christians who relate with Him being at rest like Mary. All we will end up doing is having pity on ourselves for being over-worked while others just sit at the Lord's feet like Mary.

[21]   John 4:14; John 7:38;

In all the three stories, Mary prioritizes as first the relationship she has with the Lord while Martha constantly serves Him. In all the three stories, Martha is the *giver* while Mary is constantly the *receiver* from the Lord. Let us look closer at each of the three instances:

When their brother died

When Martha heard that Jesus was on His way, she _went_ to meet Him. In this way, she was giving /serving Him with a welcome, yet Mary was _called_ by Jesus; so she received an invitation to meet Him. You see that even though they both met Him at the same place, the experiences were different: Martha _initiated_ the meeting; therefore *she _gave_ to the Lord*. On the other hand, Mary was _invited_ by Jesus to meet Him; therefore *she _received_ from Him*.

When Mary anointed Jesus feet

Martha was serving the Lord but Mary was at His feet anointing Him. Here we see Mary not doing a normal thing or rather the unexpected. As she was normally expected to be serving the lord with Martha, she instead went for a perfume that she had kept and anointed Jesus feet with it. Her actions demonstrate that she was so closely related to Him that she had an insight about the timing of the anointing of His body.

Your works will be graced with insight...!

This is later revealed after the crucifixion when women go to Jesus' tomb with perfumes and spices to anoint His body on Sunday morning, only to find that His body was no longer there. So they missed out on an opportunity to anoint it. All in all, Mary did not. She was the only one in the whole world who ever got that insightful timing right!

When Mary sat at the feet of Jesus

Again Martha was busy serving the lord and His disciples but Mary left the kitchen to listen to Jesus teach. When Martha got upset at her sister and boasted about her hard work, Jesus was not impressed by her work as much as He was impressed with Mary's sitting at His feet and listening to Him. All Mary was doing was receiving or drawing from Jesus, which is an *art* she seems to had perfected. This is equivalent to eating the bread of life and drinking the life-giving water that only Jesus offers. Unfortunately her sister had also perfected the art of serving the Lord, which will inevitably cause stress once put as the first priority.

[22]Jesus said He did not come for us to do away with the law but he came to relate us to God. He wants us to see God as our

[22]   Matthew 5: 17-20; John 5:19-47; John 14:6; Matthew 11:27

Father and to deal with God as we would with our earthly fathers; expect from Him, and draw from Him. In so doing, we honour Him and not ourselves.

This relationship is just like between a father and a son or daughter; the child looks up to the father and trusts that whatsoever daddy says is 'the real deal' and without a doubt knows that he is his father. To the child, there are no limitations as to what the father can do and so the child is constantly asking and receiving from the father. The gratuitous smile and excitement that the child expresses upon receiving gives the father so much joy. This connection is reasonably why daddies spoil their children with gifts all so often.

Now come to think of it … would it not be weird for a child to constantly be the one who tries to provide for his or her father? Of-course it would be weird, stressful and also arguably impossible. How can a five year old put food on the table, buy a car for the father, and go to work in lieu of the father? A child like this would miss out on the father's love and would exhaust his-/her-self trying to do the impossible. Oh how miserable would he/she be…! Odd as this may sound, it is literary and practically no different from our status quo whenever we seek to *give* religiously to God like Martha, instead of gratuitously *receiving / drawing* from and relating with Him like Mary did.

'Religion'- versus - 'Relationship' in Marriage

Since your husband is as Christ is to you, therefore the same concept applies to your marriage as well; that *relationship* should supersede *religious service*. In marriage, <u>*religion*</u> is all the *good* advice a woman is given by her mother and fellow community women on how to '*take care*' of her husband and children.

Take care: To take care is to carry a burden on your shoulders; so the more you take care of your family the more weight you feel on your shoulders, which results in stress...the mother of all illnesses. That is why Jesus said, [23]"...cast yours cares on me...my burden is lighter."

You probably can relate with some part or all of the following advice entirely:

"Cook your best meal every day for him and make it your business that he eats at least 3 meals a day; therefore make breakfast, pack lunch for work and cook dinner; Keep the house spotless clean at all times; Make sure he always has clean and perfectly ironed clothes to wear; Take good care of his children - feed them well and keep them clean..."

---

[23] Psalms 55:22; Philippians 4:4-9; 1 Peter 5:7; Matt 11:28-30

Yes, a good wife should care for her family but at the top of her priority should be the nurturing of the _relationship_ she has with her husband. As Jesus said:

> "but just one thing in needed. Mary has chosen the right thing ..." – Luke 10:42.

...that very relationship my dear friend is the same 'one thing needed' in marriage.

There are things that are needs in marriage while others are wants, be it in the physical marriage as in between you and your husband, or in the spiritual marriage between you as the a Christian (the bride of Christ) and Jesus. What Mary was doing by relating with Jesus is a need, while what Martha was doing is simply a want.

Likewise, there are some very busy wives out there and I hope you are not one of them; busy with work, the kids, cooking, keeping the house clean, shopping ... the list is endless and yet they do not do enough of the one thing that they are supposed to be doing, which is letting go of everything else just to relate with their respective husband.

I'm not saying that you should let your house look like a pigsty or to neglect your children or to order take-a-ways every day all in the name of seeking to relate with your husband. All that this is about is priorities, priorities, priorities…! It is for you to realize that relating with him should come first before all your other duties.

The sad thing is that there are many men who are married to *'Martha's* … these women are so religious in their marriage; they wake up before their husbands to prepare breakfast and lunch packs, clean the house spotless, do laundry, get the children ready for school, drop them off at school, go shopping, and some of these women go to work while others stay at home to work themselves tired the whole day.

Then when evening comes, they prepare dinner, bath the children, help with homework, tuck the kids to bed, wash the dishes, and just when the house is quiet and the husband tries to cuddle with his wife, all he gets is "I'm tired", "you are so insensitive", "you've been watching me work so hard and now you expect me to have the energy for 'that'", and some just go for "I have a headache". Just like that, the husband is pushed away and is refused the very thing that he married his wife for – "…relating and *'having relations'* with her…"

It is so hard for such a man to find anyone to help him with his problem as all his friends and relatives may always be complimenting him on what a marvellous wife he has. This is motivated by observing how well she always serves them whenever they visit and they also see their house, himself and the children always looking beautiful and well taken care of. They nevertheless miss out the part that the man is left lonely everyday as his wife occupies herself with everything else but him.

Sisters, please let us revisit this issue; if a clean house was your husband's first concern, he would have hired a cleaner and not marry you, but he married you not because he was looking for a cleaner - it was for him to have a *companion* - one who keeps him company. By keeping yourself so busy anyway, you go against God's *Word* when he said [24]"man must not be alone" ... so stop leaving your husband lonely and start paying some attention to him.

Let him come first...!

How about saying "I'm tired", or "I have a head-ache" to the laundry - the dishes - the shopping - and so on and so forth ... after having a great time with your husband? Be like Mary and like a child to the father; just be good at receiving from him and your gratitude will bring him immense joy.

[24] Genesis 2:18

With all due respect, I do not condone men cheating on their wives if they are *'Martha's*. I'm for the view that they must seek help, hard as it may be and solve the problem. But unfortunately so many men with Martha-wives winds up cheating on their seemingly perfect wives. They mostly date younger women who are still teenagers or college students. Wrong as this is, all these poor men are looking for is a woman who knows how to *receive* from him, who put him first, pays attention to him and definitely doesn't give him the "I have a headache story". Just like it impresses our Lord Jesus when we draw from him, the same applies for our husbands; it makes them feel honoured.

I have heard women lie to each other (and to themselves...) so many times saying their relationship(s) does not work out because they are so successful and it intimidates so many men. That, in my opinion is so far from the truth. What I think happens is that most of these women starve their men of attention as their personal success becomes their first priority. As for the department of receiving, they fail dismally because they carry the attitude that "I can do it for myself" and therefore miss out on the opportunity to genuinely show any gratitude. Then all the blame goes back to the man when the marriage or relationship breaks down.

Sisters, let us honour our men by *relating* with them and just like Mary, we will find ourselves having an insight about things concerning our families that everybody else would miss out on. Let us bring joy to our men and honour them by receiving well from them and showing them gratitude for the things they do for us. Let us do the only thing that is needed, and that is to *relate* with them.

Pertinent Questions

Question 1:

What led to submission being controversial in church?
Bear in mind that all the people who have abused 'submission' since time immemorial have done so in misalignment with God's *Word*. That unfortunately also includes church leaders, who would then misquote God's *Word* to make it fit with their wrong doings and misinterpretations.

A lot of abuse and forceful control has been inflicted on women 'in the name of submission' and it's no wonder why women in particular resent it and want nothing to do with it anymore.

Question 2:

Are men and women equals in the context of Submission?
Yes and *no*.

Yes, in spirit: - The [25]Bible says that men and women are equal in creation and redemption, and so each of them is required to *submit* to Jesus as their spiritual head.

No, in flesh: - [26]In marriage the man is the head of the woman, therefore women are to be subject of their husband's headship.

In any relationship that involves two or more people, there must be one person with whom the final authority rests in order for the relationship to be functional. In the context of a family, [27]men were ordained by God to have the final say in their homes. Within the same relationship, it is possible to layout the line of authority, or the so called chain-of-command in armed forces and the like.

You may relate well with, for instance, the formal business set-up or maybe at your place of work as illustrated in Figure (a) below. Figure (b) on the other hand illustrates God's intended chain of command in a marriage setting.

In most corporate organograms, you will most probably identify the main boss, with terms like *Chief Executive Officer (CEO)* and/or *Managing Director (MD)* and/or *Chairperson* being used interchangeably at the top of the chart. The main boss serves as the beacon of ultimate command / authority.

---

[25] Genesis 1:26-28; 2:23; 5:1-2; 1 Corinthians 11:11-12; Galatians 3:13; 28; 5:1
[26] 1 Corinthians 11:3; Ephesians 5:22-24
[27] Job 38: 3; 1 Corinthians 11:3, 8-9; Ephesians 5:23

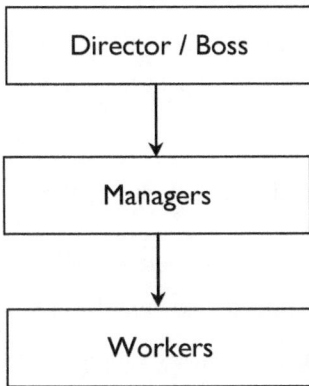
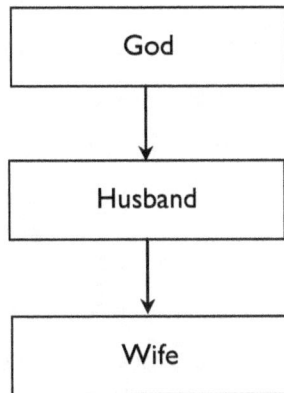

(a)   (b)

From the top-most designation and regardless of whatsoever the reference chosen by the company, the corporate authority is henceforth delegated downwards. In most cases the line-up typically takes the form: CEO - Directors - Division Heads - Line Managers - Supervisors and eventually to the general workers respectively. The order, reference titles, scope of authority, and the elaborate net-working from position to position vary from company to company.

The common thread through all organograms as tools of representation of company's management structure is that every level in the structure is representative of the level of authority. Vertical arrows are normally used to indicate the flow of authority / command from top to the bottom. They also indicate the designated line of communication. Put casually, the vertical arrows show "who-should-report-to-who". Horizontal arrows on the other hand represent the operational "ties-that-bide" and directly asserts the organizational systems theory.

You may look at the corporate organogram as a tree positioned upside down. If the roots fail to function as meant to, the entire tree up-to the sprouting leaves simply goes past-tense. Similarly in a corporate organization, should the "top-dog" be dysfunctional, then the entire organization is as good as toasted.

At this point, you may now identify with similar structures in almost every sector of your life; in your family, church, school, society-group, *stokvel*, sports-club, and so on and so forth. The functional dynamics are very much more or less the same as the corporate system. I am not sure of how your 'family organogram' looks like. Nevertheless, I simply wish to hereby share with you how mine looks like:

```
┌─────────────────────────────────┐
│  GOD-the-ALMIGHTY:              │
│  Father; Son; Holy-Spirit       │
└─────────────────────────────────┘

┌─────────────────────────────────┐
│      Director: My Hubby          │
└─────────────────────────────────┘

┌─────────────────────────────────┐
│      Manager: Myself             │
└─────────────────────────────────┘

┌─────────────────────────────────┐
│         Children:                │
│  Sandiso; Emma; Henry; Milani    │
└─────────────────────────────────┘
```

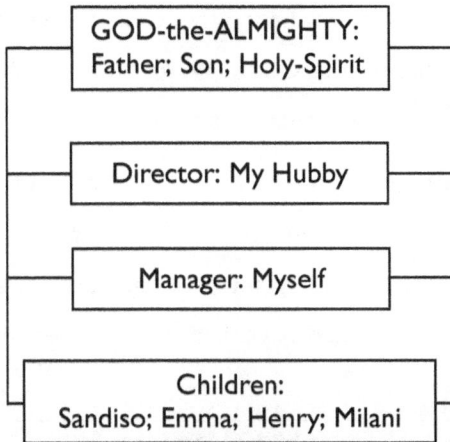

And hey, mind you sometimes I do experience bouts of overwhelming temptation to reverse the direction of the arrow between 'Director' and 'Manager'...and I think so does many other women...!

Question 3:

So, whatsoever the man says goes?

As long as it does not contradict with God's *Word*, then, and unfortunately for some ladies, the answer is a big YES...!

> "Wives should **always** put their husbands first, as the church puts Christ first."- Ephesians 5:24 [CEV].

The 'always', does not include when he tries to lead you to do things that do not line up with God's *Word*.

It is impossible that Christ would ask the church to do what does not align with God's *Word*. That is the same way a husband is required to lead his family.

With great *Respect-and-Honour* as your reference system whenever relating with your husband at the decision-making fronts, you can amicably get yourself out of a situation where you would otherwise have had to disagree with his ways or decisions.

WARNING to Women:
Do not submit to anything that is not aligned with the Word of God...!

Question 4:

What happens if your husband does not submit to God?

In an ideal situation, a Christian woman should marry a Christian man and keep away from men who don't believe in Christ, same applies when a man is looking for a woman to marry.

The Bible cautions against being unevenly yoked:

"A married woman is not free as long as her husband lives; but if her husband dies, <u>then she is free to be married to</u>

any man she wishes, *but only if he is a Christian.*" – I Corinthians 7: 39 [GNT].

As I mentioned above, 'in an ideal situation' - the better portion of our society does not live under 'ideal situations'. There are common situations where, say for instance, your husband is not a believer and yet you are one. You could be in such a situation because of numerous reasons. Nevertheless and whatsoever the case may be, as long as that man is your husband, then you have to *submit* to him provided that it fits in with God's *Word*.

Remember that God wants the best for us. So you especially need to have faith in Him to soften your husband's heart so that he can repent and so that it may be easier for you to *submit* to him. In the meantime, you have to keep on doing your part as the Bible requires of you as a Godly wife. More light will be thrown into this context as we explore the life of one of the biblical submissive women.

Pertinent insights

Jesus set an example on how to submit as He submitted to God the Father

Jesus *submitted* to God the Father 100%, and that is why He will always hold the *world record* of the only man to ever keep the 10 commandments. He fulfilled all of God's laws. He even *submitted* when he personally felt otherwise just before being captured for crucifixion; He said:

> *"Father, if you will, please don't make me suffer by having me drink from this cup. But do what you want and not what I want."* - Luke 22:42[CEV].

From Jesus' submission we can learn that even when we are confronted with situations which make it almost impossible to be submissive, we need to follow God's lead and do whatsoever His *Word* requires us to do.

The harder a situation seems to submit to,
the bigger the rewards if you do Submit, Or Else
the harsher are the consequences if you do not submit...!

The level of difficulty of a situation in terms of the required weight of submission is directly proportional to the consequences. It is a universal correlation, just like the other laws of the universe, i.e. the correlation is indiscriminate, always true, do not change with seasons, and will always prevail irrespective of your disposition, set of beliefs or awareness...!

When we *submit* mainly to God and then to our husbands, blessings are destined to fall upon us. Similarly if we if you fail to *submit*, consequential judgment will surely follow us at a proportional magnitude.

Failure to *submit* brings forth JUDGEMENT

The consequences of failed submission, for both men and women are harsh. In their different versions, I prefer to refer to them generally as judgements. Each scenario is different and each failed submission has a unique feedback. Nonetheless, the feedbacks / consequences almost have one common DNA, and that is Loss. Something dies. In a husband and wife relationship for instance, love, trust, faithfulness, honesty, patience, kindness, peace, unity, hope, passion, mutual respect, and so on are all viable candidates for the submission's chopping block. With every instance of failed submission, they wear off, they get eroded, they diminish, and eventually ... they die.

Judgment brings forth DEATH.

In the context of submission, the term death here is used generically to include other forms of death besides physical death. These forms include, among others, *emotional* (love), *social* (friendship), *psychological* (mental health), and *marital* (family) death.

'Death' as commonly perceived is associated with the spirit departing the body. Yes, that is death, and only at a certain level; there is also spiritual death - when you depart or move away from the presence of God.

This kind of death is the real death and is ultimately leads to the physical death in the long run. You must be familiar with the phrase, [28]'the walking dead'- well it refers to people who are still alive on this earth but are not born again Christians [spiritually dead] ... they live yet they are dead. That is who you and I were before we became born again. We were separated from God by sin. Therefore in order to be alive, we had to be baptized and renounce the devil and experience a spiritual birth, i.e. being born again.

God's Love - *versus* - **God's Presence**

Please do not confuse God's love and His presence in our lives. Just because a person may not be born again, that does not mean that God stops loving them. God loves us all, that is why he sent His only begotten son to come and save us from sin:

> "For God loved the world so much that he gave His only son, so that everyone who believes in Him may not die but have eternal life." – [John 3:16].

He loved us even when we were sinners...!

So, what is the difference then? When you are born again you open the door for God's Spirit, who has always knocking at your door, seeking to dwell in your heart and lead you in

---

[28] Ephesians 2:1-7; John 5:21-25

everything that you do. But when you are not born again, you continuously refuse to let God's Spirit into your heart, you refuse to let Him lead you and instead let the devil to be a resident in your heart (rent-free). In this way you separate yourself from God and all His endless goodness. In short, your spiritual being remains dead...*kaput!*

Just in case you are not saved as yet, there is still HOPE. I do hereby pray that in one way or another, God's grace do find you!

My immediate objectives

I have realized and appreciated the fact that women are very influential towards men. With that in mind, I think that if women can be awaked about their call to *submit*, then they would potentially use their influence in a positive way and inspire men to take up their leadership position in full, where they will love us as Christ loves the church; His bride.

My solemn call upon women is for them to realize how vital it is for them to *submit* first to God and then to their husbands; not to associate submission with abuse but as a means of serving. To clarify the misconceptions of submission which have led to an imbalance in life, this book has purposely been divided into 3 parts.

The 1st part is about women of the Bible who failed to *submit*, and the consequences of their failure. By analyzing their mistakes, I hope we may see where they went wrong and learn from their mistakes. Should we one day find ourselves in their position, then we may deal with similar situations in probably a better manner than they did.

In the 2nd part, we take a look at women from the Bible who *submitted* and we'll see their fruits of submission. We can look up to these women and follow their example. In both parts we see how their situation relates to what we are going through in today's life.

Lastly, in the 3rd part we get to the bottom of how women are currently under attacked by the devil, tempting them to take part in all sorts of sinful activities in a desperate effort to just get them NOT to ultimately *submit* to God.

Part 1

Women who failed to submit

Introduction

*K*ing Solomon[29] was blessed to be the wisest man to ever live on this earth; in the past, currently, and even in the future. And just to keep you in the loop, he had 700 wives and 300 hundred concubines…!

With that kind of exposure to a wide variety of characters, beauties, individualities, status, and temperaments, we can reasonably expect his insights about women to have some fair sense in them. Add on to this his experiences as a leader of God's chosen people, let alone managing his diversified portfolio of women. As for now, let us not divert into questioning whether his having so many wives and concubines was right or wrong, acceptable to God or not, a blessing or a curse … and YES, old school or new school. What I simply want is to tap into his wisdom.

This was his observation according to a book that many scholars believe to have been written by him:

[29] I Kings 3:5-14; I Kings 4:30 ; I Kings 11:3

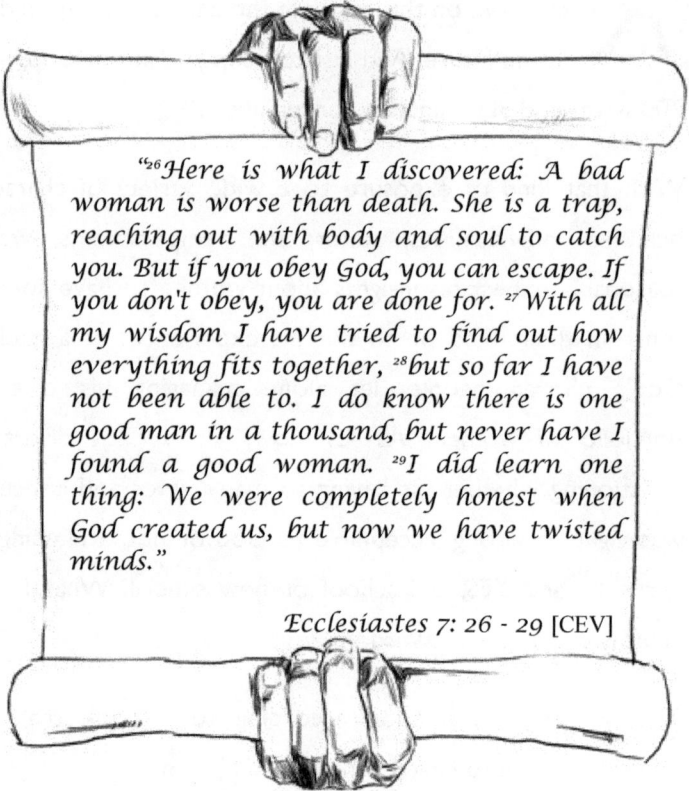

"[26]Here is what I discovered: A bad woman is worse than death. She is a trap, reaching out with body and soul to catch you. But if you obey God, you can escape. If you don't obey, you are done for. [27]With all my wisdom I have tried to find out how everything fits together, [28]but so far I have not been able to. I do know there is one good man in a thousand, but never have I found a good woman. [29]I did learn one thing: We were completely honest when God created us, but now we have twisted minds."

Ecclesiastes 7: 26 - 29 [CEV]

(1): Eve - Mrs. Adam

[Genesis 2: 21 – 23; Genesis 3]

*E*ve was probably the most beautiful woman to ever be on this earth, with nothing but perfection all over her. To top it all up, she wore the best *'designer'* gown ever, i.e. she was covered with *God's Glory*.

Eve was made by God by using the rib of her husband Adam. She was specially created for him so that she could keep him company. Before God created her, everything that she could ever possibly need was already provided for. God had even already made a husband for her. He had further provided for them a place to stay, the Garden of Eden, which He had made Himself. He had also provided for them meals for everyday, which included juicy fruits from trees that He had planted. They could eat as much and as many varieties as they wanted, with the exception of only one tree that God had warned them not to eat from.

She had nothing to fear as she was essentially the Queen of her husband and had authority over all the animals that you can imagine of. I can imagine they all feared her as she ruled over them alongside her God-ordained husband. She was well hooked-up.

As for her husband, Adam, you can just imagine how handsome and well-built he was considering that God physically moulded him. As if his physic was not enough and the fact that he could give Eve everything she wanted, he was also perhaps the most intelligent man to ever exist. He must had been a genius or even more superior; to imagine that he named all the animals that exists in this world - those that we know of and the extinct ones that were present in the beginning of creation (ALL the animals that God created) ... and all that with no repetition of names, no use of a computer or server, and no pen or paper to write on. That should give you an idea of just how smart he was. And then Eve just had to have him for a husband ... makes you feel jealous, Ha?

Come to think of how we casually think that Albert Einstein was one of the most intelligent of mankind, if not the most intelligent of all...? Yes, that is true to some extent, and with all due respect, he was nonetheless a *no show* as compared to Adam. [30]Einstein is myth-*fied* to have been able to use about 10% of his brain, which explains why he was considered such a 'genius'. This is in comparison to the average human being whom statistics claim to be using much less a percentage. Whether this myth holds some water or not, the afore-contended relative *status quo* stands.

---

[30] Wikipedia. [Online]. Ten Percent of Brain Myth. Available at:
      http://en.wikipedia.org/wiki/Ten_percent_of_brain_myth. (Accessed 7 August 2011)

That aside, the Almighty God was their regular visitor at their home - the Garden of Eden; he would come down from heaven and pay them a visit and they communicated with Him face to face ... talk about being married to a guy with connections in high places ... they knew the One who's definitely in the highest of them places...!

With the perfect life that Eve was given, she only had one restriction ... and that was not to eat from the tree in the middle of the garden. Only that. Done and dusted. Full stop...!

Amongst those animals, the snake was the most cunning of them all. So one day it went to Eve and suggested to her that she must eat the fruit that God had forbidden them from eating. When Eve told the snake that she couldn't eat it because God had said that if they eat it from it they would die, the snake, with its tricky nature, told her that they would not die but they would in contrary be able to tell the difference between good and bad.

And so after Eve looked at the fruit, seeing how tasty it looked like, she started to imagine herself wiser. She contemplated the benefits of eating the fruit. In her head I guess she thought, 'this fruit looks very appetizing, plus I'm (suddenly!) hungry – so it will fill me up and make me smarter'. Just like that, Eve gave in to the snake's temptation and ate the fruit; totally breaking the only rule she (and her *hubby*) had been given.

And she did not end there ... She also offered Adam the fruit to share with her. Adam must had been so in love with her that he also took a bite, knowing very well of the consequences that would follow. That was the beginning of sin. After Adam had eaten, they immediately were stripped off God's gown of glory and they both noticed that they were naked.

Embarrassed about what they had done, they went to hide behind one of the trees in the garden. God paid them His usual phenomenal visit. The only difference this time around was that, instead of them welcoming God and running along to meet Him, they remained behind the trees where they were hiding as if they were playing hide and seek with Him.

Noticing that they had hidden, He called out for them and asked why they were hiding. In total embarrassment, they resurfaced from their hiding place. When He asked them why they ate the forbidden fruit, they then started pushing the blame from one to the next instead of apologizing; Adam blamed it all on Eve and to God, saying:

"The woman you put here with me gave me the fruit, and I ate it." - Genesis 3:12 [GNT].

When Eve's turn came to answer, she pushed on the blame to the snake. Consequently, God banned them from the garden. As a warning of the repercussions to follow due to the *door* they had just opened, He said to Eve that she would suffer from labour pains when having children, yet she would still long for her husband and be under his rule. To Adam, He said that he would have to work very hard to earn a living (in order to provide for his family) and that one day they would finally die, turning back into soil. And finally to the snake, which was actually the devil in camouflage, God said that it would always eat dirt and crawl on its tummy. Further in a much deeper sense addressing the devil side of the snake, He told it that the offspring of the woman would later on crush its head ... literary the most 'for-sure' way of killing a snake.

Before Adam and Eve left the Garden of Eden, God slaughtered an animal and made cloths for them using the animal's skin. Just like that, they were chased away from the garden. God then put His angels to watch over the Garden's entrance because next to the forbidden fruit was the tree of life. By so doing He was protecting them from eating the fruit of that tree because it would result in them living forever in sin with no hope of being reconciled with Him.

Eve later on gave birth to two boys; Cain and Abel, one of whom eventually ended up murdering the other. In order to further relate to the 'cradle of sin', you may revisit the Biblical account of events as they unfolded around the first sin according to *Genesis 3*. Just as God had said, many years later on, an offspring of Eve crushed the snake's head; that's what happened when Jesus was crucified, delivering us from the Devil's grip once and for all.

From the onset, and to my understanding, Eve was meant to *submit* to both God (regarding His caution about the tree in the middle of the garden) and to her husband, Adam. God created Adam and Eve, and as such, had full authority over their lives; they had to *submit* to Him. Eve was formed out of one of Adam's ribs, and likewise the chain of command flows.

Let us now dissect Eve's encounter in the context of submission and dig out some valuable lessons from her failure to *submit*.

LESSONS to learn from Eve's life

Lesson #1: Studying and memorizing scripture

God instructed them not to eat from the tree of knowledge; to Eve's full awareness, they were to eat from all the other trees except for the tree in the middle of the garden. She even knew the consequence (death!) that would befall them in case they failed to honour God's instructions. So, was it by virtue of attitude, forgetfulness, or just taking things for granted that led Eve to submissively fail dismally as she did?

It is thoughtfully very draining to concur with the fact that when the serpent paid Eve a visit, she got deceived to the effect of obeying the snake's word. Notice she had to choose between the two 'words'; God's *Word* or the serpent's word - as we now know how the story continues, Eve chose the snake's word.

If you do not familiarize yourself with God's Word, you will be deceived.

The snake (the devil) deceived Eve by simply sowing a seed of *doubt* in God's *Word*. Despite knowing God's *Word*, and in their case an express directive from God, she for a moment entertained the possibility of another version of the *status quo*. She got tricked and she failed...!

Since the times of the garden to this day, the devil tempts us in ONLY these three different routes; the fresh, eyes, and pride. All the tricks that the devil has up his sleeve are written in the first letter of John:

*"For all that **is** in the world - the lust of the flesh, the lust of the eyes, and the pride of life - is not of the Father but is of the world. And the world is passing away, and the lust of it; but he who does the will of God abides forever."* - 1 John 2: 16 - 17 [NKJV].

Lust of the fresh infers to what the sinful self-desires; *lust of the eyes* infers to what we as human beings see and want, while the *pride of life* infers to everything in this world that people are so attracted to and proud of. That is why it's so imperatively important to study God's *Word* at all times so that whenever the devil coins his tricks, we will be able to discern them and have God's *Word* ready as our reference in order not to fall prey.

Unfortunately for Eve, it does not seem like she had sufficiently familiarized herself with God's *Word* and it's no wonder that she was deceived. By the devil purporting to know much more than Eve already knew, she must have felt inadequate in her scope of knowledge. However, she definitely knew enough of what she needed to know ... that if they did eat the fruit of that tree in the middle of the garden, then they would die. Take note here that her knowing God's express directive was insufficient at the face of devil's foul-play. In other words:

Knowledge - Submission = Disaster !

We later on see the devil using the same three tricks on Jesus in the wilderness, yet Jesus could not be deceived because He not only knew the *Word* but also *submitted* to it. [31]Remember that to each of these three tricks His response was, 'it is written...', referring to the scriptures.

What about us?

We really need to read our Bible, study it all the time, and memorize verses, not for show but to use them when the enemy tries to deceive us. [32]The Bible advices us to be alert and of sober mind because... 'Your enemy the devil prowls around like a roaring lion looking for someone to devour'. So let us be warned of the fact that he is relentlessly after us.

Warning: Do not ever rely on your own strength to defeat the devil. Make use of the Word of God.

The good news is that if we know the *Word* of God, then the devil stands no chance with us.[33]Jesus used only the *Word* of God until the devil gave up for that time.

Why memorize?

Can you imagine the devil pulling his tricks on you while you

[31] Matthew 4: 1 – 11 [ESV]
[32] 1 Peter 5:8
[33] Matthew 4: 1 – 11

are at work, and then as the good Christian you are you tell yourself, 'as soon as I knock off work, I'll rush home for my Bible to find the verse for this trick.' I'm sorry to disappoint you my dear but that just will not cut it. What if Jesus pulled off such a stunt in the wilderness and said, for instance, 'as soon as I'm off this mountain, I will go and look up the scriptures with which to defeat you'. Seriously, we would probably not have been delivered from sin as it is today. I thank God for Jesus' familiarity with the Word.

Temptation is not a sin but yielding to it is;
Even Jesus was tempted!

On a consoling note, we need not stress about failing to remember the scriptures whenever we need to because the Holy Spirit will remind us when that time comes; we just need to do your part of knowing the scriptures. Jesus promised us:

> *"The Helper, the Holy Spirit, whom the Father will send in my name, will teach you everything and make you remember all that I have told you."* - John 14: 26.

Lesson #2: Keeping outsiders outside

Mrs. Adam should have exercised her authority over the snake by putting it to its place when it tried having a conversation with her. She shared authority over the animals with her husband, Adam. But instead, she lowered her standards by communicating and taking advice from the snake despite her being superior to it. She could have even punished it for initiating a conversation with her towards contradicting the ultimate authority; God's instructions.

What about You?

Have you also lowered your standards in your marriage for instance? Perhaps like Eve you have taken ideas from outsiders, third parties with whom you have engaged into a conversation about matters of your marriage. I am talking about matters that you should be seeking God's advice for and discussing with your husband (or wife as the case may be), instead of seeking advice from your friends. Yeeeeap...! - you know what I'm talking about...!

As much as you love your friends, when it comes to issues concerning your marriage, it's wise to communicate with God and your husband, and to keep outsiders (your friends and enemies alike, relatives and anyone else) where they belong, that is, *outside* of your marital affairs.

Most of the time outsiders deceive you, with terrible advice which may be harmful to your marriage. This is of-course with the exception of a professional marriage counsellor, who may be your priest, pastor, psychologist, or psychiatrist. These are people who can be allowed, and are more often than not, trained to help out whenever problems arise in relationships. Nevertheless, and at all times, God should take first place. Seeking for God's *Word* and direction, by praying and reading the Bible often and looking for scriptures that deal with whatsoever situation you may be going through, is the best choice. Remember even the marriages of pastors, psychologists and psychiatrists also get wrecked up ... but God's *Word* prevails...!

As much as possible, always remember that God's *Word* is sufficient to take care of every situation that you will ever face in your life. Eve heard the *Word*, but she chose to disobey it. Yet if she had obeyed it, all of her needs would have been taken care of forever and she'd probably still be alive today, living a sin free life.

That one *Word* from God was enough to give Adam and Eve eternal life on earth with total dominion over all the animals. I say eternal life because in that same garden was the tree of life, which God intended for them to eat from since he never told them not to eat from it. He later on had to protect it from them after they had sinned. This is because He did not want them to live in sin forever.

[34]The Bible says that the snake was the sneakiest of all the animals in the Garden. For that reason we may excuse Eve for stooping so low and having conversation with the snake. It probably approached her in a very charming way that for a moment she forgot her position. Somehow in some way, the snake made her an offer she could not resist.

What if Eve's response to the snake was like, "Okay Mr. Snake, your idea sounds cool, but let me discuss it with my husband first and then I'll get back to you"? Chances are that her husband would have reminded her of what God had said, and this would have most likely brought her back to her senses. Who knows? - He probably would have killed the snake or reported it to God and gotten it banned from the garden.

And come to think of it ... are you aware that Adam was not deceived; only Eve was. He sinned knowingly, choosing to follow his wife! On the same note, remember Eve was designed or meant to be a pillar of support for Adam; a companion, an assistant, a helpmate. Consequently, it can be deciphered that she could not support him without being submissive to God and him. Contrary to the expectation, Adam *submitted* to his

[34] Genesis 3:1

wife, Eve, regardless and at the expense of his prior knowledge of God's warning and *prima facie* call to *submit* to God.

You cannot support your husband if you are not submissive to him.

What a formidable power it takes to influence someone to do something wrong knowingly? - Eve was used as a "carrier" to propagate devil's deception. Even to this very day the devil reckons with, and still uses the *ka*-woman power to lull men into sinning ... even knowingly...!!! Notice that nothing happened until the moment Adam ate the forbidden fruit. This asserts the man's position as the God-ordained head of a family unit.

How about You?

Are you using advice that was given to you by an outsider without first consulting with your husband?

Consulting with your husband does not mean that you cannot think for yourself. As matter of fact, you honour your husband when you discuss things through with him before implementing them in your life. And believe you me; it more often than not works out best for the team than otherwise.

Recap

Each one of us has had a forbidden-fruit-moment(s) in our life. The very instance we *doubt* God's respective *Word* about such moment(s), we thereby generously open a window to Devil's attack...!

(2): Jezebel

[1 Kings 16: 29-34; 1 Kings 18, 19, 21;
2 Kings 9; Revelation 2:19-25]

A princess by birth, Jezebel was the daughter of King Ethbaal. She later on became queen of Israel when she married King Ahab. She was a devoted worshiper of her foreign gods, mainly *Baal* and the goddess *Asherah*. In order to please the gods that she worshiped, human sacrifice used to be given to them. She even offered one of her sons as a sacrifice to these gods.

As an Israelite, Jezebel's husband was a worshipper of the Most High God, *Yahweh*. With time, Jezebel influenced him to worship her gods, which in God's eyes resulted in King Ahab being the worst King Israel has ever had.

At some point King Ahab wanted a piece of land that was next to his palace and he made an offer to the owner. The owner refused to sell him the land because it had a sentimental value to him; it was priceless as he had inherited it from his father, having been passed down from generation to generation. This upset King Ahab. When he told Jezebel about it, she sent out letters to all the king's officials. She signed the letters with the king's seal as if the king had written them himself. In the letters, she stated that they should declare the following day a holiday of worship and then publicly accuse Naboth, the man who refused to sell the land to the King as having refused to respect the day and then kill him as punishment for disobeying the King's order.

The officials did as they were told and Naboth ended up being murdered. When the news got to the Palace, Jezebel received the message with joy and told the King to go and claim ownership of the land as the owner was dead. Without questioning an obviously foul-play situation, the King went ahead to take ownership of the land.

Because of all these, the Lord God sent His prophet Elijah to alert King Ahab that He was of aware the murder that had taken place for them to possess the land and He pronounced His judgement. But because the King was remorseful, his respective judgment fell on his children and all his descendants. As for Jezebel, she got her judgment in due time; her servants threw her out from the palace window and dogs ate her flesh, so much that only her remains were buried.

After her husband died, their son Jorum became the King. He ruled for only two years, after which the Lord sent His prophet to kill him and all of the descendants of Ahab. So it all came to pass as it had earlier on been prophesied.

Now let us look deeper into Jezebel's character in order to understand and relate to who she really was.

Jezebel's Character Traits

In an article written by [35]Edwin and Sophia Christian, hereby adopted and adapted with permission, the authors invite us to take a deeper look at the character traits that go along with the spirit of Jezebel. This is on the ground that it is much more than what meets the eye and can be extremely difficult to discern for the untrained eye.

According to the authors, there are certain characteristics that always seem to follow these women (and men). The authors have therefore made an effort to map some of them for us so that we may be able to recognize them in our family, job, school or church, or anywhere else we may go; we can only spot the Jezebel spirit when we understand her personality or the character traits underlying her skin. For a more elaborate insight into the subject, you may consider reading Parts 2 and 3 of the series.

Character trait #1: I am right...!

The very first, and probably most outstanding quality of a person with a Jezebel Spirit, is their undeniable, ever-present need to always be right! They are not humble people who seek the input of others, but have an unquenchable desire to "win"

---

[35]   Edwin and Sophia Christian. [Online].Available at:
       http://instituteoflove.net/index_files/Page022.htm [Accessed 10 May 2010]

over you in everything.

The worldly term for the spirit of Jezebel is 'malignant narcissism' for which there is no cure. Some traits of narcissism include: excessive self-love; firm conviction that he or she is better, smarter, or more talented than other people; becomes irritated when other people don't automatically do what he or she wants them to do; thinks most criticisms of him or her are motivated by jealousy; regards anything short of worship to be rejection; often complains of being mistreated or misunderstood; has fantasies of doing something great or being famous, and often expects to be treated as if these fantasies had already come true.

Character trait #2: The "Chameleon" Spirit

The second thing, highest on the list, is the "chameleon" spirit she possesses that allows her to *appear* a certain way, but not actually *be* that way. She will adapt to her surroundings to seem like a loving, charming, and even peaceful person, all the while trying to get a hold of your soul. She will appear to blend in, and suddenly, out of nowhere, stick her tongue out, and swallow you up, by verbally attacking you.

The Jezebel spirit is born out of witchcraft and is designed to destroy the host (which is the body it lives in), the spouse, children, family, relationships, marriages, the church, the prophets of God, and the body of Christ in general, in every crafty and subtle way possible.

Character trait #3: Hideous influence

The third aspect is her use of seduction, deception, and manipulation to control your mind, your actions, and your destiny. She wants to see how far she can involve herself into your life, how far you are willing to allow her to go.

Jezebels usually come in two categories; the active, and the passive - or as is / has been said - the high-profile, and the low-profile. The high-profile, active Jezebel is the woman who is the leader of the home, including everyone in it. She is the one who "wears the pants" in the marriage / family, the overbearing, bossy, in-control, in charge, dominating woman, who is outspoken, bold, and militaristic.

The low-profile, passive Jezebel is the woman who controls the husband and family "behind the scenes". She has a meek exterior, and no one would guess that she has the family in a head-lock, quietly controlling, manipulating, and destroying peoples' lives. She is soft-spoken, seemingly submissive and nice on the outside, and only the closest family knows the truth about who she really is.

Jezebel hates children, especially her own, but it takes great discernment to discover it. Women with the Jezebel Spirit tend to treat their children cold and distant, rarely showing tears or emotion. She likes to make sure they don't get any sympathy, because she hates weakness. She doesn't show much love or affection – genuine hugs, smiles, and affirmation are a rare gift. Usually, her children are merely treated as pawns in her game of control and achievement of power. She uses conditional love to ensure her children's subordination. In this way, they will always strive for her attention and approval, and she will glory in it, only for her own self-gratification.

Jezebel will often mix religious terms and phrases to appear godly, but her life doesn't produce godliness. Following her life and example will lead to rebellion, darkness, anger, and strife.

Often times, you will find a Jezebel woman involved in various types of teaching activities. Not only will you find her in religious settings, but also in places such as schools and various types of counselling. The reason for this is simple; people with a Jezebel spirit have an insatiable desire to exert their influence onto other people. The spirit within them drives them to want to *reproduce* themselves and their teachings to other people. They like to be highly involved in people's personal lives, getting up-close and intimate, making people confide in them. Then they become important, needed, and wanted, just the way they like it. Satan places them specifically in teaching positions so that they will impart a distorted and untrue message to people, and thereby cause more spiritual and mental darkness to come upon their lives. People may be in a bad condition when they come to a Jezebel, but they leave worse off than how they came.

Jezebels are masters of the "blaming game", and are extremely clever in gaining sympathy for themselves by producing convincing arguments for her cases, usually portraying themselves as fair in their assessments. They will twist and turn information to better fit them, even if it involves lying and crying, anything to make others be the responsible or guilty ones.

Jezebel does not truly forgive people who offend her. She keeps track of all past offenses, and she uses them to her advantage when she sees the need for manipulation. Her love is always conditional, making you know of the things that please her, so if you do not comply, she will reject you.

The Spirit of Jezebel also produces sexual imbalance and perversion in the children. We have seen many examples of rebellion and extreme dark and obscure behaviour in children and teenagers of mothers who possess the Jezebel Spirit. The family around them does not seem to understand why the children choose rebellion instead of becoming "normal" like everyone else, not knowing that it is actually not always a choice of conviction, but rather a direct influence by the distorting spirit of Jezebel operating in the family. The control the children are under causes them not to develop as strong, individual, healthy human beings, but causes perversion and confusion, and sexual immorality.

Children of Jezebels can also fall in the exact opposite category, being overly well-behaved, submissive, pleasing, passive, and shy of conflict. They can be recognized by their fear, lack of ambition and self-esteem, many times rather wanting to take the blame for everything upon themselves, instead of searching for justice.

LESSONS to learn from Jezebel's life

Lesson #1: Confusion - Versus - Peace

A Jezebel spirit will never admit any fault or wrong-doing. If you plan to confront the Jezebelite with something, you can be totally clear about your problems, and your list of concerns, and yet come out on the other end, totally convinced that you were the only one at fault. The mighty dark cloud of confusion that surrounds the Spirit of Jezebel makes you give up, and give in to her demands without proper reason. You don't even know what hit you, you just don't have the strength to fight her, and you may even feel a sense of relief for achieving peace with her, not realizing the prize you are paying is compromising for the sake of peace.

The spirit of Jezebel brings about a tremendously powerful confusion that can make you doubt everything you stand for. After your first few confrontations, you learn to stay away from coming even remotely close to suggesting correction. You find out that you are not strong enough to stand up against it, and start becoming passive. This kind of passivity is what King Ahab suffered from when he looked the other way instead of confronting the wrong his wife, Queen Jezebel, was doing.

When Jezebel heard the news, she said to Ahab:

> *"You know the vineyard Naboth wouldn't sell you? Well, you can have it now! He's dead!"* **So Ahab immediately went down to the vineyard to claim it."** - I Kings 21:15-16 [NLT].

Because of King Ahab's passive negligence of Queen Jezebel's wicked actions, we have the term "Spirit of Ahab" which is the "perfect" counterpart to Jezebel. He wants to remain innocent, but is anything but innocent in the eyes of God. In fact the Bible says Ahab was an evil man, possessing the same persecuting spirit as his wife, as he mocked the prophet Elijah and called him intimidating names:

"So it's you, is it - Israel's troublemaker?" Ahab asked when he saw him. - I Kings 18:17 [NLT].

Jezebel is calling Jehu names, mocking him and comparing him to another murderer:

"When Jehu entered the gate of the palace, she (Jezebel) shouted at him, "Have you come in peace, you murderer? You are just like Zimri, who murdered his master!" - 2 Kings 9:31 [NLT].

Remember, Ahab's passivity cost him everything. The Bible says he sold himself to evil. In other words, it's not only through Satan worship we can sell our souls, but also, when we sell our souls to worship another human being, who will drag us into a life away from God.

"No one else so completely sold himself to what was evil in the LORD's sight as did Ahab, for his wife, Jezebel, influenced him." - I Kings 21:25 [NLT].

Lesson #2: **No Peace Around Jezebel**

I believe we have to understand that dealing with the Jezebel spirit will never be peaceful! One has to give, and that is certainly not going to be Jezebel if she has her way. A Jezebelite does not respect anyone, and certainly not someone of lesser authority than herself. She will *never* humble herself and help find a way to make things work. Things have to be <u>her</u> way, or no way at all. King Jehu, the warrior, knew that there was no achieving peace; no compromise that could be made with Jezebel, only a violent counter-action could stop her:

> *"King Joram demanded "Do you come in peace, Jehu?" Jehu replied, "How can there be peace as long as the idolatry and witchcraft of your mother, Jezebel, are all around us?""*- 2 Kings 9:22 [NLT].

Lesson #3: **The *Ka*-Woman Power**

Unlike God, we as human beings tend to judge things by what we see on the outside. This tendency has led to numerous innocent people being charged with crimes that they never committed. They are nevertheless found guilty simply because some evidence points at them as having committed the crime and that evidence happens to be excellently projected and defended by the contextual prosecutor. Evidence such as fingerprints and / or 'eye witness' testifying to having seen a wrongly accused person at the crime scene has often been taken to suffice for a prosecution. Unfortunately the judge often only relies on the evidence presented 'under oath'. Similarly, some actual offenders have been acquitted on basis on 'lack of sufficient evidence'. This evidence is grossly external (physical) and is not always right.

In contrast, God is always a better Judge as He looks for internal evidence that does not necessarily manifest in a physical form, for instance the thoughts and deep-seated feelings of a perpetrator. God in that way always makes the right decision revolving around any situation. That is why His ways of judgment are always mysterious to us mortals. It takes God's wisdom for people to be able to function like God and discern things from within, thereby evaluating situations in a better way.

Owing to our shortcoming of only assessing things or situations from eternal evidence, human judgement has led to men being considered to be more powerful than women. Women have always been perceived as the weaker sex, which is a big mistake because nothing else can be as far from the truth. As further elaborated in the chapter on Mary (PART 2 of this book), our physical internal organs have greater power of influence over our lives than the external organs. Our bodies have a higher resilience to pain related to external organs than that associated with internal organs. As such, the internal organs more easily push us around than external organs, and sometimes frog-match us anyhow as we seek to broker peace with them. It is by no mistake that these organs are 'internal' and therefore protected by the 'external' ones.

With that frame of reference in mind, remember the woman was taken from the man's inner part ... the man's rib. There are two aspects to this. Firstly, the ribs serve as reinforcement for the chest zone of a human body, just like pillars in a house. They further enhance protection of the inner more delicate body organs like the heart and lungs. As such the woman is analogically meant to 'reinforce' the husband in a marriage context. From a similar stand point, the spot where the rib came from became weaker. Put differently, the man naturally and analogically has a 'soft spot' with reference to a woman.

Secondly, the woman was moulded from a rib that was an inner part of the man's body, the same inner parts that we said have greater control than external ones in reference to the entire body. This symbolically means that the woman has great power *over* the man. She can control him, not particularly by 'man-handling' him but by influencing him ... she can 'order his steps'...! That is just her God-given strength that cannot be taken away from her. Nonetheless, God requires her to *submit* to her husband.

Why have so much power, yet be expected to *submit* to one with less power? This, in my opinion is because of the fact that a woman would not even require to have faith in God for her to influence a man. Her natural ability alone is sufficient enough for that. In contrast, she will have to rely on God's ability for her to be able to *submit* to her husband, empowering her to act from a place of faith, in love, and great humility. She gets to praise God in so doing.

You do realize here that the woman's influential power does not go to waste but rather bears fruits towards submission to God. Furthermore, we see that the woman has been given the *potential* role of a shepherd; by her submission, she can lead a man to God by influencing him to follow God's ways.

Bear in mind though that 'power', in this context of submission cannot interchangeably be used with the term 'authority'. By the woman having greater influential *power* over her husband, it does not mean that she has greater *authority* over him.

On a parallel platform, if your 'Boss' at work is a woman, it means she has the authority over you, whether you are a man or a woman. She does not necessarily have to exercise her *ka-*woman *power* over you for you to *submit* to her. In case she ever did exercise such power, you would still be entitled to exercising your own discretion at will. This is completely different from an instance of her exercising her *authority*, in which case your choices are succumbed to corporate interests, rather than being a mere issue between you and her. And please do not get me wrong ... this does not in whatsoever sense mean that the *ka-*woman *power* has not often been camouflaged as corporate *authority* by some women...!

It is worth noting here that *submitting* to God, which leads and empowers a woman to *submit* to her husband, is perhaps the most liberating experience that a woman can ever have. This is because, in so doing, the woman gets to be honoured with the rewards that she would otherwise only fantasize. These rewards include true love, peace, joy, unity, prosperity, health, life, fruitfulness, wisdom, and so much more.

As a peek preview of just how big the rewards can be, our LORD Jesus Christ set a perfect example for us in how honourable it is to *submit*. He had all the power to do as he pleased; He had the power to stop His crucifixion and free Himself from the agony and humiliation that it came with. But only with humility and love for us that He was empowered to *submit* to God's will and Kingdom's interests.

The results...?

God honoured Him with the highest position ever; He is now seated at the right hand side of our Father and will soon return to judge everyone, both the living and the dead. I know not of a higher reward than that. The woman is similarly called upon to exercise her influential power in humility and love for her husband.

As you can recall, Eve for a moment doubted God's *Word* and used her God-given power to influence Adam into eating the forbidden fruit. Here we see a God-fearing man being at the palm of the woman he loves. Rightfully so, just imagine ... if a Godly woman can mislead a man, how much more mess then will an ungodly woman deliver to a man...?!

Even the God fearing women who are submissive still do have an underlying potential within to be a Jezebelite, simply waiting to be unleashed at anytime, anywhere, and whenever the faith in God is lost. An excellent example that we can relate with is Sarah, Abraham's wife (to be addressed later). She was a very submissive woman but at one point, just like we all go through moments of doubt, she doubted! She doubted the *Word* of God coming true, the promise that she and her husband (Abraham) were going to have a child. So for a moment, she stepped out of faith in God and relied on her natural power; she influenced her husband into sleeping with her slave. You may notice here that, a God fearing man as he was, Abraham gave in to Sarah's feminine power.

Like all the women who failed to *submit*, Jezebel chose to use her woman power for her own pleasure rather than for the sake of God's Kingdom. She influenced her husband, King Ahab, to worship the idol gods that she preferred, thereby turning him into being the worst King that Israel ever had. Ahab went along with Jezebel's ways like a puppet, even in the obviously foul situation relating to Naboth's piece of land. She had him at the palm of her hand, controlling him as she wished. All women who choose not to *submit* to God's authority follow in Jezebel's footsteps.

As women, God has entrusted us with great power and it is in His *Word* that He guides us on how to use it responsibly. It is upon us to choose to *submit* to Him, to our husbands, and to all His earthly ordained authority that He has placed in our lives.

Dear Jezebel,

Without a doubt, you discovered what woman power is and used it to your advantage. Unfortunately you did not use it for the glory of God as it is meant to be the case.

One might imagine that God wanted nothing to do with you, given your record of turning your husband into being the worst king that ever ruled Israel. To the contrary, God had abundant grace on you, being true to His Word - 'where sin abides, grace is more available' [Romans 5:20].

The Bible says in Revelation 2:21 that God gave you plenty of chances to repent. To my imagination, God must have used the same method He uses for every sinner, i.e. shower them with unconditional love, make available His Word, offer forgiveness, and give the gift of righteousness and abundance of life.

God's arm of love and deliverance was all available throughout your life, but you chose not to receive it.

Clearly Elijah was one of the ways that God sent for you to receive His Word. You could have learnt so much from him and your woman power would have worked for the better. Your influence would have been great and significant in a positive manner. Worshipers of idol gods would have been saved … surely you would have influenced a good number of your fellow worshipers to believe in the true God with your testimony of God's grace in your life.

It is too late for you now, but I can only pray for those of us who are still alive, especially those who are possessed by the 'Jezebel spirit', that we may be more discerning and wiser in order to make better choices than yours.

Disappointed,

Pypie.

(3): Queen Vashti

[ESTHER 1]

... LIBERATED WOMAN, Arrogant woman ...!

*Q*ueen Vashti was married to King Xerxes of Persia who lived in his capital city, Susa. He ruled 127 provinces from India to Ethiopia. In the third year of his rule, he hosted a lavish party for his high ranking officials from all the 127 provinces. The party lasted for six months, during all of which days he showed off his wealth.

Soon after that party, he hosted another one; this time everyone in the city of Susa was invited, no matter who they were. It lasted for a week. He had provided so much food and he ordered his servants to make sure that everyone ate and drank as much as they pleased for the entire week. The best deco was used at the palace, making it look exclusive, for instance, exquisite golden cups were used to serve the wine. While everyone was having fun outside the palace, Queen Vashti too had hosted her own party inside the palace.

On the seventh day, the King had feasted and drunk so much wine and was merry with all his guests. He had once again showed off all his wealth and was ready to now show off his most valuable treasure in the palace. So he asked seven of his servants to call for Queen Vashti and ask her to put on her crown so she could parade for their guests and show off to everyone what a very beautiful wife he had.

Sadly, Queen Vashti refused. Even after the seven King's servants begged her to honour the King's request, she still stood her ground. The servants eventually gave up on her, went back to her husband the King, and informed him that she refused to come to him. The King was very angry. Disappointed and embarrassed about his wife's behaviour, he consulted with his advisors who advised him to expel the Queen from the palace, strip her off her title of being a Queen, and to replace her with a humble, obedient woman.

So Queen Vashti was stripped off her title and chased out of the palace. She was soon replaced by a submissive, God-fearing, and humble young lady named Esther who became the new Queen of Persia.

Queen Vashti's background

This woman is an excellent reminder of how an evil seed, if not dealt with, can cruise on through generations. She was just like her father and grandfather...! Queen Vashti was born to Babylonian royalty; her father was Belshazzar and her grandfather was Nebuchadnezzar, the one who destroyed Solomon's temple in Jerusalem and drove Jews to exile.

Her father continued from where his own father, Nebuchadnezzar, left of in his hatred for Jews and his disobedience to their God. It is said that he (Vashti's father) strew a party and commanded revellers to drink from the holy vessels of the temple and then praise the gods of silver and gold. At that moment a large unattached finger appeared and started writing on the wall "MENE, MENE, TEKEL, UPHARSIN", meaning:

"God has numbered the days of your kingdom and brought it to an end. He has weighed you on his balance scales, and you fall short of what it takes to be king. So God has divided your kingdom between the Medes and the Persians". - Daniel 5: 25 – 28 [CEV].

That same night, invading hoards of Persian and Medes attacked: Vashti was the only survivor! But the spirit of conquest that had doomed her father lived on intact within her.

It's said in the [36]Talmud that Vashti abducted Jewish women, forced them to parade naked for her and forced them to work for her on Sabbath. She used to belittle the Jewish women as they proved to be untouchable by serving someone higher than the monarchy.

---

[36]   Megillah 12

To be "liberated"

The term liberation relates the act of setting someone or something free from oppression, confinement, foreign control, or whatsoever other form of constraint. It also informally relates to the act of taking unlawfully something that belongs to somebody else. In the context of submission, liberation can either be exercised: (1) expressly and freely without reservations, or (2) out of concession, and in some cases, (3) in rebellion.

In the first instance, there is no second party in the equation; a person will exercise his or her choice(s) at his or her own discretion, the effects and / or consequences of which actions will be borne by the individual *per se*. A simple yet excellent example for this category will be the choice of whether or not to eat food. The choice is yours. If you eat, it will be beneficial to your health. If you do not, you will starve, and no one will feel the hunger on your behalf. To put it in back-street language, the effects and / or consequences of your choice(s) are your own 'donkey'…!

The second instance entails some compromise involving two or more parties. Any choice made is, in itself, a fruit borne of mutual understanding and in due consideration of other party's interests and dispositions. A husband and wife decision making process is a very profound example for this category, whereby the choice(s) made by the one of them do affect the other, be it directly or indirectly. Similarly so are the effects and / or consequences. Liberty in this context implies considered actions within the framework of consensus of understanding, which sometimes will be at the expense of personal interests, or for the sake of the other party(ies).

The third instance relates to wilful, deliberate, calculated, intentional, stubborn, informed, in-subordinating, and spiteful choice(s). It surpasses any form of goodwill. It respects no boundaries, rules or statutory laws; it seeks to stretch, strain, wring, and strangle any defined normalcy. It may involve one or more parties, and so does the effects and / or consequences of the respective choice(s).

I fully do support liberated women. After all I consider myself to be a liberated woman, liberated by Jesus Christ who paid the full price to set me free from being oppressed by sin. Nevertheless, I do not identify with women who are struggling to pamper their egos (pride) and then regard themselves as liberated women. Such was the profile depicted by Queen Vashti.

Pride

I do not feel worthy to even teach about this 'lesson on pride' because I know that I am still a student in the very lesson. You have had your own relevant experiences and I therefore hope you will hereby relate well to my raw insights.

While researching on pride, I got a shock of my life by awakening to the fact that I have lived all my life under the influence of pride and I did not even realize it. At some point I thought I had learnt the lesson, only to discover that I had not really soaked it in.

Self

The first composition that we had to write at the start of every grade from Grade three to seven was titled "Myself". With each year passing-by and graduating from one grade to the next, I noticed that my composition was getting longer and longer and it was easier for me to express my views. In Grade seven, I could literary fill-up two pages just writing about "Myself"…! Little did the teachers know that they were in actual sense destroying us by this kind of composition. So from an early age, we were taught that you can define yourself by your life experiences and diverse status, which creates the illusion of self and unconsciously leads one into being a slave of pride.

So, who are you?

The shortest answer that most people give to this question is their name(s). For instance in my case it would be Pypie. However, Pypie is <u>NOT</u> who I am. That is my name... actually my nickname. The author of this book, mother of 3 wonderful children, a wife, and my parent's daughter, a friend ... and the list can be endless BUT all these are simply <u>what</u> I am. None of them is even close to <u>who</u> I really am.

Albert Einstein (one whom we consider to have been a genius of all times), is [37]cited to apparently had figured out who he was when he spoke of "a grotesque contradiction between what people consider to be my achievements and abilities, and the reality of who I am and what I am capable of". By virtue of truly understanding who he was, he remained humble and egoless.

Remember that in the beginning when God created human beings he said:

"Now we will make humans and they will be like us..." - Genesis 1: 26 [CEV].

---

[37] Eckhart Tolle. [2006]. *New Earth*. Penguin Books, Page 84.

So God created humans to be like Himself. If we are like God, the question then is: who is God? God is an eternal spiritual being. He existed in the beginning before everything else, and continues to exist to eternity. Now when He made us in His own likeness, He gave us His spirit (by breathing into Adam). Just like God, we are spiritual beings and from the time God created us, we will forever exist into eternity like our creator. The only difference is that while we are on this earth, we will live in a body. Nevertheless, the real us remains the invisible one, the spirit man.

Contrary to the afore-going understanding and just like Queen Vashti, most of us human beings struggle with the knowledge of who we are. Because of this ignorance, we let pride rule us in making us think that we are who we are not. We identify ourselves and others by what we / they do, where we come from, colour of the skin, our social status, achievements and so on.

"My people perish from a lack of knowledge ..." - Hosea 4: 6 [KJV].

There are numerous references in the Bible about how God is against pride. That simply indicates that He is aware of how destructive pride is; also called "Ego" / "Self". Can you see that by having pride, one is not aligned with God's *Word*?

The [38]Bible severally says that one (the self) must die in order to live. Sounds like a paradox at face value, yet it is not. If pride results to death, then what brings or restores life? Eliminating pride / ego / self does bring life. He meant that we should substitute the 'me', 'myself' and 'I' with the likes of 'we', 'our' and 'they'. Let it be more about God's Kingdom and other people as opposed to being all about you. He said "Serve one another", which overflows into, say, *be mindful of one another, watch each other's back, love one another*, and so on.

At the realm of being fruitful, having children is the best thing that can ever happen to a person. They truly are such a blessing in so many ways, one of them being the help in the 'elimination or suppression of self'. Unlike when we are living single and life is all about us, having children kills the 'self' especially when they are young; we totally forget about the ourselves as they become our number one priority. We indirectly get the hang or taste of serving others just like Jesus implored. We get to really learn how to love unconditionally, to share, to forgive, to carry the next person's burden, and to give with no strings attached.

Nevertheless, pride will not go down the drain without a fight,

---

[38] John 11:25; Matthew 16:24-25; Mark 8:34-35; Luke 9:23-24; John 12:24; Romans 8: 10-15

which is why I hereby assert that having _children_ is one of the best ways to kill 'self' besides _marriage_. For a marriage to thrive, an indispensable trait in the relationship is the persistent effort to consider each other's interests, feelings, opinions, and otherwise in a selfless way. However, people often get on-board the divorce train as soon as 'self' is threatened. They immediately start feeding the 'self' by blaming everyone and everything else except for 'self'. It is no surprise then that divorce has evolved into being such a formidable prevalent vocabulary in our dialect.

Unlike in _marriage_, you cannot 'divorce' your _children_; once you have them, you are stuck with them for life regardless, which is also partly why the rate of abortions is sky-rocketing. 'Self' is trying to protect itself from being eliminated. God said, [39]"...Multiply..." knowing very well that for us to multiply, it would take us being Godly, viz, 'dying to self' or 'being selfless'.

How 'self' will protect itself / fight back

Back from hospital with your bundle of joy you might think life will only get better; that you'll enjoy it with your baby and _hubby_. Reality check: the bad news is that that is yet another castle in the air ... not if 'self' can help it.

---

[39] Genesis 9:7

Children below the age of 1 year, especially in their first three months, put their parents pride to a rigorous test. With their need for attention 24 / 7, they threaten both parents' ego and they will nail down that 'self' if given a chance. Ladies, you will agree with me that after having a new-born baby or even other children thereafter, men do change, at least to some noticeable extent ... hey?

Why?

In my opinion, it is a primarily recourse of the 'self' earnestly trying to restore itself. For instance, your husband will start complaining about how much you are spending more time with the kids than with him. Some men will even use it as an excuse for cheating in the name of seeking attention. But beware it is not the man who is seeking your or otherwise attention; it is his pride itself, feeling left out ... the 'self' feeling starved. This I think is perhaps one of the best times to emulate [40]"...Father, forgive them, for they do not know what they are doing...".

Some men will start resenting the child because he / she 'steal-the-show'. Why? After arrival of the kid(s), the equation is no longer just about them parents, but more about the kid(s), especially in the early stages and pride cannot handle that.

---

[40] Luke 23:34

In mothers

Knowing very well that there is no way out for mummy with respect to prioritizing the baby, the father can at times ignore the child and do nothing for him / her. He can even *crash* on the couch or guest room when the baby needs attention at night. In contrast, there is no way out for mummy but to forget about her needs and care for the child. I say there is no way because, in my opinion, it is not a natural phenomenon for a mother to neglect or abandon her own baby. The selected instances when that ever happens can be attributed to either genuine medically explainable causes, e.g. postnatal depression, or 'self' related reasons, e.g. anger towards the baby's father, fear of inadequacy to provide for the baby or any other form of fear, shame or whatsoever other 'self'-related excuse.

In general, 'self' is very much aware of the mother's predisposition relative to her baby and will fight for its survival the best way it knows how. The more demanding a child is, the more 'self' fights back. To a great extent, I believe that this partly contributes to the constitutive number of mothers being treated for post-natal depression. And hey, guess what the remedial treatment for post-natal depression is? Firstly we have *medication* – most of the medication cuts off the mother from breastfeeding as part of the prescription … and what does that interpret to for the baby? = Less attention for the baby and limited maternal bonding.

Secondly we have *counselling* – affected mothers are 'advised' to take time off the baby and find support such as hiring a nanny, or get help from relatives and friends … the moment that advice takes effect, 'self' lives on…!

One may rightfully argue that these two remedies are a 'necessary evil'. Nevertheless, bear in mind that the two remedies would not be necessary in the first place were it not for the devil's hideous attack on life. It can equally and rightfully be argued that the roots of post-natal depression go all the way back to 'self-awareness.' Simply take note here that ALL these so called reasons and causes for neglect or abandoning of a baby by a mother are part of the devils weapons against proliferation of life and has been addressed in full details in Part three.

Just for the record, I do identify with this road of *'self'-versus-child* too well. After having my third baby, I even went to the extent of suffering from bouts of 'panic attacks'. Guess what healed me? – Going back to a working-mother lifestyle – they immediately disappeared after I started paying more attention to 'me' rather than the kids.

Queen Vashti's pride

She was a princess by birth, a non-Jew princess at a time when Jews were slaves. So she thought very highly of her-'self' and defined herself by her circumstances. So when her husband King Xerves called her to model for his guests, the very Jewish man that she already looked down upon because he used to work for her father [Talmud], she must had induced so many questions into her mind ... maybe for instance, does he know who (actually what) I am? Who does he think he is? ... I just can't help but wonder what was going on in her mind when she refused. Whatsoever her immediate thoughts and / or questions were, her pride just set in, squarely...!

It seems like nobody warned Queen Vashti that [41]Pride comes before disaster and arrogance before a fall. We see her demonstrating her pride when she refuses to heed the King's request. Her pride refused to allow her to come out of her 'self-bubble' in the call of submitting to the king's request. Nothing but pride led her to refuse going out to her King and husband. And thanks to that very pride, she lost her position of being the Queen. Further, she then probably felt like she lost her whole being because she did not know who she really was.

[41]   Proverbs 16:18 [CEV]

This is someone who knew herself as royalty from being a princess and later on being a queen. Following her act of contempt, it must had been very hard for her to experience being 'kicked out' of the palace, the only kind of residence and royalty she would probably identify with since her childhood. In today's slang, it would sound like being transitioned 'from a Queen to a *Hobo*'...!

In life, there is always an opportunity to make choices, especially the choice of life. It is recommended severally in the scriptures, [42]"Choose life ... not death". So even for Vashti after making the wrong move and facing contextual judgement, she still had a chance to *choose life*. She still had the opportunity to eliminate *self* and learn from her mistakes. Her expulsion experience could potentially be an opportunity for her to find her true identity. She could get to know who she really was while she owned nothing and had nobody on her side, realize that nothingness could take her to place of no fear, no anxiety, nothing to prove ... a place for her to just be...! - and while there, maybe, just maybe ... she would find her true identity.

'Self' is like a parasite; it kills its host.

On the other extreme hand, Vashti could have chosen death and thereby leave the palace with so much feelings of

[42] Deuteronomy 30:19-20; 2 Kings 18:32; 1 John 5:10-21; 1 John 3:14

bitterness, anger, hurt, self-pity, and disappointment. She could have died believing that she had been cheated, in one way or another blaming the King, life and / or God. All these feelings would practically be an unconscious way of feeding the 'self', the very thing that led to her contextual 'death'.

In marriage

As long as we enter into marriage not having substituted the 'I'-s with 'WE'-s, the divorce rates will keep on going so high that the idea of even getting married will be really dreadful. We cannot expect happy marriages when we enter into them with a predominant 'self' – 'pride' – 'arrogance'. Just like Vashti, you too my dear sister can go from being the Queen of your household to being a divorcee, thereby joining many of those who blame it all on men or otherwise. No...! – Just beware that it's not the man. It is not even you. It is more often than not the *pride-in-action*.

Princess attitude

Vashti's father was a King; I can imagine that she must had grown up thinking that she was a very important person by virtue of getting used to seeing servants around her father's palace attending to her every demand. Through her marriage to the King, two things happened. Firstly, she became a Queen, and had to *submit* to the King as a subject of his kingdom. Secondly, she became a wife and had to *submit* to her husband. But Queen Vashti failed to do both...!

In my opinion, you can't afford to get into marriage having an 'I am a princess' attitude. Otherwise, how will you *submit* to your husband? How will you serve him and your children, with that kind of attitude?

Princess attitude in marriage won't work.

A great part of me really feels sorry for her because of her background. Again in my opinion, psychological help would probably have done her lots of good. She was raised under abnormal circumstances; to witness so much hatred from (her) family towards fellow beings (Jews) would never have been healthy for her mind as a child. And to add salt into injury, she witnessed the death of everyone she could identify with. One can only imagine what that kind of experience can do to the human mind, especially that of a child.

Your past experiences can affect your present moment and future in a negative way unless you deal with it.

She grew up seeing and hearing about the hatred for Jews. She did not know any better. Am I excusing her for the terrible things she did. No! Certainly not! I am just acknowledging the roots of her rebellious attitude. Vashti isn't the only one with a hard and seemingly unfair background; there are so many of us who come from dysfunctional homes and yet we do not make *being-mean-to-others* our full time job!

We cannot deny though that our background does play a big role at influencing how we behave as adults. We need recognize whenever and however our past does creep into our here and now and yet come scenarios. Only then can we be able to seek for help towards streamlining our frame-of-reference.

Beware that it is more often than not very difficult for us to recognize this effect of our backgrounds all by ourselves. This is partly because it somehow feels normal as one gets to be brainwashed when still very young. Consequently, even the bad experiences may unfortunately be learned or perceived as being part of the norm by default. That is why I believe it is good and advisable for couples to get to know each other well before getting married; including sharing with each other about their individual past experiences and background settings. Keep no secrets...! And in general, hone your communication towards building up a common reference system.

Queen Vashti failed to *submit* in 3 ways:

(1st) Submission to God

Queen Vashti did not *submit* to God and she was not impressed about the way Jewish women showed their submission to God by honouring the Sabbath. She never honoured the Sabbath as the *Word* of God requires. Instead, she even forced those who did to dishonour it by forcing them to work on the Sabbath day. Pride simply could not let her *submit* to God. She rebelled...!

(2nd) Submission to her husband

In the [43]Talmud it's stated that when her husband called her she said that 'once you were my father's stable boy...'. She had no respect for her husband and all she saw in him was her father's boy. She rebelled...!

(3rd) Submission to the King

We are meant to honour and respect appointed leaders in our lives. We are to follow their instructions as if those instructions were from God provided that they are not instructing us to disobey God himself. A good example was set by [44]Daniel and his three friends (Shadrach, Meshach, and Abednego). Daniel

[43]   Midrash Rabbah
[44]   Daniel 3 & 6

prayed to God instead praying to the King Darius, while his friends in a separate occasion refused to worship any other gods except the Almighty Living God even after the King had ordered everyone else to do so.

LESSONS from Queen Vashti's life

Throughout the analysis of Queen Vashti, I hope we have been able to learn: (1) *Childhood background* - the effects of our upbringing, i.e. how our backgrounds can be limiting yet we have to deal with them, (2) *Ordained authorities* - the necessity of *submitting* to ordained authority: God, your husband, King, President, Pastor, and so on, and (3) *Self* and *Pride* - the power of *self* and *pride* and their unforgiving grip on us mortals.

Dear Vashti,

I do not fully understand why you decided to be so disrespectful to your then husband, by refusing to go to him when he called you.

I wonder if you were aware that he called you because he wanted to show you off to his guests as his treasure in the palace. After showing off with all the great things he owned, he saved the best for last, YOU!

I don't agree with the way you treated your Jewish servants, but I have the impression that at that time you were struggling to put your ego under control, which eventually cost you a lot.

I hope that at some point you got the help you needed, and awakened to the greatness of submitting to any God-ordained authority in your life.

Sincerely,

Pypie.

(4): Bathsheba

[2 SAMUEL 11]

Bathsheba was married to one of King David's soldiers named Uriah, a Hittite. At one of the times when the soldiers went to fight to protect the nation, her husband too was fighting in the battle and therefore she was left alone at their home. It so happened that King David had returned from the battle and was resting in his palace. At about the same time, Bathsheba decided to take a bath, which was a religious act according to the custom of those days but the place where she took a bath was visible from the palace's roof. So after King David had rested, he went for some fresh air at the roof-top of his palace and then, lo and behold…! - there was Bathsheba, naked…!

Responding to the heated signals caused by what he had just witnessed, King David ordered one of his servants to fetch Bathsheba to come to the palace. His wishes were granted as Bathsheba was fetched. Then King David had sex with her and sent her back home when he was *done with her.*

A couple of weeks later, Bathsheba discovered that she was pregnant. Since her husband had still not returned from the battle field, she knew without a doubt that she was expecting the King's child. So she wrote the King a letter informing him of her discovery. The news made him panic.

After thinking things through, David ordered that Bathsheba's husband be relieved from the battle field. This was in the hope that Bathsheba's husband would go to his wife and sleep with her so that when the pregnancy would eventually show up, he would think it was his own child.

To King David's disappointment, Uriah did just the opposite; upon being relieved from the battle field, he went straight to the King's palace and when night-time came, he slept outside by the palace gates. When King David tried convincing him to go home to his wife, he said he could not enjoy sleeping at the comfort of his home knowing very well that his colleagues were still in the battle field.

Upon realizing that his hatched plan would not work, King David then sent Uriah back to the battle field and told his commander to place him at a dangerous spot and not to field him so that he could be killed. Well, David's 'Plan B' worked and Bathsheba was left a widow.

After King David got the news about the death of Bathsheba's husband, he proceeded to make Bathsheba one of his wives. The child she was expecting was a boy and when he was six years old, he became ill and died. Later on she had another son who was a blessing from God; his name was Solomon, who eventually became the wisest and richest King of Israel. Just as a by the way, Bathsheba also later on mothered Nathan, the one in the seed-lineage of Jesus (Corinthians 14:4).

LESSONS from Bathsheba's life

Lesson #1: Confused submission

We all know that we have to *submit* to our leaders (parents, husband, boss, pastor, king, president, and so on), but God is always the one we should *prima facie submit* to. If what our leaders want us to do is not aligned with God's *Word*, then we should not do it. This is because it would mean disobeying God in order to please man, which is not of God.

What if your boss wanted to have sex with you? Would you do it in the name of submission? In the context of submission, it means nothing the fact that David was a King; Bathsheba was a married woman, yet she just had sex with him without being forced. The story would have been different if David had raped her. It is, however, written that they had sex. Maybe she even felt honoured for the King to want to have sex with her.

Lesson #2: Dress code - DECENCY...!

Don't tempt men to sin by exposing your body to them.

David did not plan for this to happen; he was just strolling on his roof top, and then there she was … naked! It is common knowledge that men's lustful thoughts are easily provoked when they see a 'beautiful' woman wearing a revealing outfit, or even worse when she is naked.

This implicitly means that most of us have committed Bathsheba's sin whenever we show off our cleavage or reveal more skin than we should. Hey! - You are free to wear whatsoever you want but make sure your freedom does not lead you into being part of a sin.

Of course, I am aware that there are some morally-challenged men out there. I strictly do not condone their acts of sexually or verbally abusing women, claiming that the particular women deserved it because of what they were wearing. No, that is not what I am talking about here. I am talking about exposing the better part of our bodies, for example the breasts and / or thighs to the world, and then God-fearing, married or unmarried men happens to see us and get excited. Such men will probably not do anything to us but hey, they will be tempted! So, where does that leave us? It means we go around tempting men, good and bad ones alike, whenever we wear inappropriately revealing clothes. I believe that, as God-fearing women, we can do much better than being *traps* or *temptations*.

[45]Remember that this is the very same David who trusted God so much that while he was still a young boy, he killed Goliath the Philistine giant at a time when all the Israelite army had *chickened-out* from the challenge. [46]This is the same David whom God made a covenant with to the effect that the messiah would come from his blood-line. Obviously this was a man of God, yet just the sight of a naked woman stripped off all his anointing for a moment and he ended up being an adulterer and then a murderer.

David defeated a strong giant and killed wild animals but just the sight of a naked woman brought him down on his knees!

Ladies, can you see just how much power we have in us; I mean … David had the courage to face a giant but had no strength to fight his own lust towards a naked woman…!

Do not let fashion cost you your holiness

[47]The Bible encourages that women should pay more attention to their inward beauty by fearing the Lord, and wear that instead of making the outward beauty a priority. If following

---

[45]   1 Samuel 17
[46]   2 Samuel 7:10-13; 1 Chronicles 17:11-14; 2 Chronicles 6:16
[47]   1 Timothy 2:9; 1 Peter 3:3-4

trends for us comes at the cost of tempting all and sundry men passing our way, then maybe we should reconsider how you present ourselves to the world. After all, fashion is of this world and as God believing women we are not to be transformed of this world. Rather, we are to be ambassadors of transforming it. It is up to us as God-fearing women to set the trends, not to follow them. It is our call to make it fashionable to wear decent and appropriately covering clothing. Let the rest of the world learn from you and I.

What does the Bible say…? I suppose we can hereby back ourselves up with the proclamation that we are not the tails but leaders. It is about time that we start living our daily lives as guided by the Scriptures.

And hey, mind you I am not saying that you now should dress-up like a tired, rundown, elderly lady. There are so many outfits out there that will make you look fabulous without you having to expose much of your flesh to the world, especially your thighs and / or breasts, otherwise fashioned as the "cleavage".

Your body is God's temple

Each time you dress up, remember that you are furnishing God's temple. Yes, you are God's temple, His spirit lives in you.

I promise you that if you start perceiving your body as God's temple, there will be so many positive changes that you will see because you will then honour your body as a vessel that carries God's Spirit. You will keep it clean, polished, in a safe place, preserve it, and restore it. You definitely will not be comfortable with just about anybody coming close to it because you will finally fathom the full measure of its value; Priceless…!

Dear Bathsheba,

Reading about how dedicated your husband was to his work, I realised that he might have been a typical workaholic. From that perspective, I realized how starved of love and attention you must probably have felt in your married life. This makes me actually wonder what your intentions were when you took your monthly bath at such a visible spot.

Were you hoping that David would see you? Was it a hatched plot or just sheer coincidence? Whatsoever the case, God's grace found you - you were blessed with four sons and entrusted to raise the world's wisest man ever; King Solomon.

Moreover, your son Nathan got blessed to be in the line of the messiah's seed carrier. This means that the seed passed through you. Regardless of how your relationship began with King David, God's grace was sufficient to pick you up to be one of the women whom God honoured with carrying of His seed.

Once again I say...God's grace found you Sister...!

Yours in Grace,

Pypie.

(5): Lot's wife

[GENESIS 19: 1-26]

*T*his lady was married to Abraham's nephew, whom Abraham (the father of all nations) had chosen to travel with when God told him to leave his family. Her husband's roots were from as far back as to Noah – the man who built the Ark. His family tree was as follows: Noah – Shem (one of Noah's sons) – Abraham and Haran (brothers) – Lot (from Haran).

Before they got settled down, Lot's wife had had the opportunity to see up-close the relationship between God and Abraham. As God blessed Abraham, her husband Lot got a share of his blessings and he also prospered. But there came a time when their herdsmen started fighting and as a solution, Abraham decided that they part ways and settle down in separate locations. Her husband Lot chose that they go and settle with all their possessions in Sodom; a land that was looking good, near the river and had good pastures.

Even though the place was looking good, it was full of very evil people. They constantly disobeyed God. As a result, God decided to destroy all of them. Before doing so, however, He sent His angels ahead of Him to see if Sodom was as evil as it was rumoured to be.

One day as he was sitting at the city gates, Mrs. Lot's husband saw two men approaching from out of town. Realizing that it was already late he invited them to spend the night at his place. He persuaded them because at first they had refused but then later on agreed. What he didn't know however was that they were God's angels, sent by God.

As the angels spent time at Lot's home, they shared with Mrs. Lot's family about God's plans to destroy the city. They even gave them a chance to inform their relatives of the trouble set to come so that they would be saved. But no one believed Lot about it.

In that very evening, after Lot had cooked and served the two men (angels) with food, the Sodomites lived up to their reputation by coming to harass them, wanting to sexually abuse them. In a frantic effort to save the visitors from Sodomites' pervasiveness, Lot offered those Sodomites his virgin daughters instead as the situation became really bad, with the men trying to force their way into the house. Then the angels struck all those Sodom men blind, thereby preventing them from finding their way to the door.

When morning came Mrs. Lot and her family were given a chance to escape the destruction that was to befall Sodom. For a moment, they just froze when it was time to run, so much that the angels held them by hand and led them out of the city. When they got to a safe place, the angels told them to keep running and not to look back until they were out of the city. So they all ran for their lives. For some strange reason(s), Mrs. Lot looked back before they got out of the city and she immediately turned into a pillar of salt.

Lot and their two daughters kept running till they got to the place where they settled. Sometime later, and possibly out of a high probability that they would never get married as they had settled in a distant land, the two daughters got Lot very drunk and took turns in sleeping with him, which for both of them resulted in pregnancy.

Mrs. Lot's privileges

We often look at what went wrong for her, how harsh her judgment was and forget about how privileged she was in her life compared to all the other people in Sodom. [48]Mrs. Lot had a first-hand experience of walking alongside Abraham and seeing God's manifestations in his life.

In this particular incidence, she was warned by the angels about the disaster which was to fall upon Sodom. She was even physically pulled out of Sodom as she lingered when the

[48] Genesis 14: 16

morning came. She personally experienced God's Favour and yet she still dishonoured God's *Word* by looking back.

The [49]Bible says that when the son of man comes, things will be just as they were when Noah lived. People were eating, drinking and getting married right up to the day when Noah went to the big boat ... This indirectly warns us about the unreadiness in which people will be when Jesus comes back in His second coming. We are further warned we should always remember Lot's wife.

What if God spared her life?

What if God spared lots wife? Perhaps that would mean an unfinished job since she carried Sodom in her heart. She would possibly have easily infected others with the Sodom's evil spirits.

At face-value it looks like God's judgment fell on her, i.e. it may look as if God was angry at Lot's wife and as a result turned her into a pillar of salt. However, the way I see it is that her predicament is similar to Adam and Eve's warning with respect to the forbidden fruit because of its resultant effect of leading to their death. When they ate the fruit, they initially died spiritually and eventually died physically.

---

[49] Luke 17: 26-27

So when the angels warned the Lots not to look back, the instruction was not just of their own understanding but from the *memo* they had received from God. As we are already aware, the angels were only acting on the Word of God, delivering God's message just like they often do to us. God's love towards her and her family is clearly evident in that she was warned early enough alongside her other family members.

It should be easy to relate this troublesome situation to other biblical accounts where God miraculously rescued so many of his servants, for instance, Daniel in a pit of lions (Daniel 6) and Shadrach, Meshach, and Abednego (Daniel 3) in a fiery furnace. However, we need to recognize the fact that these people landed into such situations as a result of their acts that were fuelled by faith, which is a capsule Love. They were under God's wings, in love and obedience to His Lordship. Unlike these people, Lot's wife acted on fear; a capsule of lack of faith in God, often driven by human desires, and fully inspired by the devil.

An act of fear is an invitation to death in all its forms, while an act of faith is an invitation life.

If fear were a consumer product, the devil would literary be the sole producer, and owning up the entire supply chain. His brand would probably be FEAR™. As it is right now, he thus far can only inspire us to be afraid, thus resulting in a state of a *curse* and not of *blessing*. Thank God His Grace has us covered and He always has a way of reaching out to us.

Why did Mrs. Lot look back?

Nobody knows for sure!

She may have just been curious to see what was happening despite an instruction to the contrary. Have we not all been curious at some point about matters of the worldly life, even after we received salvation? If that was her case, then her '*curiosity killed* ... more than just ... *the cat'*. Once you let go of your evil ways the best thing to do is to press on and look forward, or else you may face the risk of falling forever, like Mrs. Lot.

Attachment to the Worldly things

From a physical human anatomy's perspective, if you look back while walking, and even worse while running, you stand the risk of stumbling, and most probably getting injured. To a great extent, so is the even greater risk from a spiritual perspective. Physically ahead of Mrs. Lot's family as they run was 'safety' at face value. On the other hand, material wealth and lifestyle that they had identified with for quite a long while was dwindling and perishing behind them.

In my opinion, Mrs. Lot's looking back therefore shows us just how much she was attached to, and / or in love with, the worldly possessions. Unfortunately for her, she stumbled into another 'style' of being – a pillar of salt.

Beware: "…Know ye not that the friendship of the world is enmity with God? Whosoever therefore will be a friend of the world is the enemy of God. - James 4: 4 [KJV].

Before looking back, I think her thoughts must had been racing back and forth, trying to digest the events that were unfolding since the last couple hours ... all the wealth she was leaving behind, her 1st class lifestyle, her social life (friends), experience with the angels, and the like. As she was running away, her heart was still stuck in Sodom, until her body gave in and she looked back, thereby disobeying a direct command from God's angels not to look back.

Trusting in the LORD

God doesn't reveal all His future plans for us but He wants us

to trust Him and just follow His lead, knowing that wherever it is that He is taking us, He has worked out a good plan for us:

..."For I know the plans I have for you," declares the LORD, "plans to prosper you and not to harm you, plans to give you hope and a future." - Jeremiah 19:11 [NIV].

Yet that seems impossible for us to believe; we want Him to show us first what lies ahead, we want to have a sneak-peek preview into our future or else we just refuse to move. We get stuck onto looking into our past and remembering the good old times we've had and how we did this and that. While engrossed in such moments, we fail to realize that we are literary spending our time absent from the present. We are either worried about the future or trying to re-live the past and not paying any attention to the present moment.

"...Trust in the LORD with all your heart and lean not on your own understanding; in all your ways submit to Him, and he will make your paths straight..." - Proverbs 3: 5 - 6 [NIV].

LESSONS from Mrs. Lot

Lesson #1: Do not tolerate evil

The onus is on you and I not to tolerate the evil that is going on in this world because we risk being infected by it if we do, let alone being affected by it. We need keep as far away from it as we possibly can. You see, as Christians we are to minister to the world with our lives and shower her with love. However, that does not mean we should tolerate her evil ways.

Going to church is not enough; the people we spend our time with, the kind of shows we watch, the kind of entertainment we permit for ourselves and the kids alike to have ... all these do matter because they are of great influence. Even where we raise our kids, i.e. the surrounding wholesome environment ... just look at what happened to lot's children!

Transcending Judgment OR Fate?

For doing the only thing that they were explicitly directed not to do, Mrs. Lot was turned into salt immediately...! Even though her children escaped, you can decipher that they needed a lot of counselling because they most likely were already mentally disturbed especially from the previous night's ordeal.

I am not sure of what you see to have proliferated in their mind with respect to their moral-values reference system. Nevertheless, what I see is a situation where God's grace saved them, yet their mother's spirit of doubting God's *Word* transcended beyond herself all the way to her children ... another generation. Just like their mother seemingly doubted and acted against the angels' command, they too seemingly doubted God's providence. They did not trust that God would work out a plan for them to get married, just as He had worked out a plan for their salvation. [50]They thereby sought to assist God by drugging their father with alcohol with the hideous motive of having sex with him.

To a great extent, I also think their social experiences in Sodom as they grew up must had been contaminated, yet somehow subdued. An indicator to this was the fact that they were engaged to men who were Sodomites, yet on the other hand, they were being raised in the priesthood of a God-fearing man; their dad. Just how do you, in your right mind, drug your father into having sex with you, for whatsoever the excuse? I earnestly hope you do get to understand my concern here.

Don't fool yourselves. Bad company will destroy you.
I Corinthians 15:33 [CEV].

It is debatable as to whether this behaviour was as a result of a transcending spirit from their previous life and environment or just sheer fate. Whatsoever the case, it is our responsibility to examine our own hearts so that we may be aware of and acknowledge our sinful nature that leads us to disobey God especially in His seemingly *smaller* commandments. In addition to that, we need trust and rely on His ability to herd and guard

---

[50] Genesis 19:30-36

us from evil that we often get exposed to in this world we are in.

Lesson #2: Grace and Salvation

It was by grace that the Lots were saved from the destruction that befell Sodom. The entire family was saved as they set out of their home, dragged by angels. However, Mrs. Lot seems not to have absorbed the full measure of that FAVOUR. The only restriction they were given as they set off for safety was to not look back. Simple and clear! She took it for granted, thereby knowingly or unknowingly watering it down.

An analogy can be drawn between the account of events that embraced Mrs. Lot's family on one hand, and the New Testament's teachings on the other. Salvation in the context of Mrs. Lot's family was not only in the physical sense, but also in a spiritual sense. To start with, it was not Lot or any member of his family that chose to be saved; it was God that chose them, a magnificent exemplification of God's Grace. Just imagine ... one family ONLY out of an entire city. The only eminent difference between them and the rest of the families in Sodom was that, at least, Lot as the God-ordained family leader was submissive to God's Word.

Secondly, just as Salvation today gives eternal life, their lives were saved from the fire of judgement that befell Sodom.

Thirdly, they had to accept the salvation, that is, the request to run away from the city; mind you Lot had gotten a chance to ask the fiancés for his daughters to come along but they refused.

Fourthly, the two points that marked their salvation were mutually exclusive, that is, they could not go to the place of safety and still hold on to their former life-style and possessions in Sodom. Similarly, our Salvation today is a mutually exclusive journey in that one cannot be born again and still hang on to the old ways of life. It would be like choosing to live for Christ and for the devil at the same time. This latter contention is affirmed by the aftermath that befell Mrs. Lot the moment she tried to tap into where they were coming from by way of looking back. At that point, God's grace on her simply fell off and got replaced by judgement, viz, her turning into a pillar of salt.

As of today, you probably have come across some Christians doing all sorts of sinful things on the account that they operate under the new covenant of grace and not of the old covenant of the law. Therefore they knowingly sin and then plead for the blood of Jesus to wash off their sins. We ought to realize that that is just like trying to manipulate God's mind; trying to play witch with the Almighty God.

Take note that it is not just God's judgement that befell Sodom and Gomora; rather, God's grace was at hand in the first and foremost instance. It was only after refusing God's grace that judgement proceeded. Notice the chance that was given to Lot for him to inform his would-be sons-in-law of the imminent horror – that in itself was *grace-in-action*. If only they had believed him, they too would have most likely informed their own immediate beloved ones. As we can imagine, each beloved would have informed his or her own other beloved and the chain-reaction would have probably proliferated to reach all corners of the city. In no time, the entire city would have been saved from the fire. As the account has it, they just could not believe. In as much as safety from the fire is represented in the physical sense, their failure to believe relates to a spiritual level.

The same scenario is no different from our scenario today. We live all our life with God's grace at hand. Nevertheless, if we keep rejecting, we risk dying in the dark ... having not been saved and awaiting judgement. Jesus came to set us free from operating under the law. He made it possible for us to go back into operating under God's grace. All we need do is let go of our worldly ways, repent our sins, and believe in Him.

Remember that before the law, our ancestors were operating under grace; it did not matter how much they moaned - God still provided for them and protected them, but they thought that they could gain Favour by merit. Then God gave the 10 commandments, just to awaken them to the fact that they could not be perfect - They did, as much as we still do today, NEED His *Favour* to survive. So God sent His only begotten Son, who was the only one capable of fulfilling the law, then He set us free and gave us salvation for free. So today we can be saved and operate under His *Favour*.

Then what about the 10 commandments?

The [51]Bible says that He will write the laws in our hearts. In essence, see that we do not throw the commandments away; they come even closer to us, only that this time they are NOT meant to show us how incapable we are, but rather to lead us into a life of abundance and appreciation of God's grace.

YES! - Salvation is free to us but please beware that it did not CHEAP. It cost God His ONLY son - He had to watch Him suffer on the cross just to save us from spending eternity in hell. As such, we cannot afford to ever cheapen it by

[51]   Hebrews 8:10; Jeremiah 31:33

disregarding God's commandments in the name of being blood-bought Christians.

'Half loaf'- versus - 'Full loaf'

Submit fully to God's *Word*. Let us not come in half-heartedly; [52]Jesus cautioned against the attitude of receiving salvation half-heartedly, being lukewarm - No! - Either we are *hot* or *cold*, or else we will perish.

Salvation is the greatest gift, greatest miracle on earth. It is priceless, given for free, and yet not cheap. I pray that you may receive it with 'both hands' and cherish it with all your heart because it is the best treasure you will ever have. It is very sad to realize that some people, out of ignorance, do weigh its worth with or against money and material possessions.

If we reflect back abit, we realize that the Lot's were worldly rich. It is no surprise that they froze when it was time to leave in the morning. Instead of running for their salvation, they must had struggled in digesting the thought of how they were about to let go of all their wealth, and probably fame, and just leave without packing and just leave everything behind; for what? They might had been reconsidering things here even though it was clear that if they did not leave, they would be destroyed.

---

[52] Revelation 3:15,16,19; Hebrews 6:12; James 4:8

We stand no ground to judge them because we are still doing the same thing in this world today. Just like them, salvation has been offered to us - to run to a place of safety and there is not much time left. The world and its system (our Sodom) will be destroyed soon. Ooooh Yes! - There is no difference! - [53]We too have been warned and the message is the same: 'Jesus is coming soon ... are you ready?' [54]The world is about to be destroyed with all its possessions and a safer place has been prepared for us.

The pertinent question is: Who will you be in this story? I hope you will be like Lot and realize that salvation is greater than all the wealth you have amassed or accomplished to build, rather than being like the Lot's wife, who looked back as she still longed for worldly ways, things and pleasures. Keep your eyes on the LORD and trust that He has *got your back*.

Despite being married to a God-fearing man, and through whom she had been blessed and considered worthy enough to literary witness God's Favour in her family's life, Mrs. Lot lived a double lifestyle; one of being like a typical 'church goer' and the other of being in love with worldly things. It's like one person trying to drive two vehicles at the same time ... IMPOSSIBLE ...!!!

[53] Revelation 16:15; Revelation 22:12; Matthew 24:1-51; Hebrews 8:28; John 14:3
[54] John 14

Recap: Jesus is coming

[55]The *Word* of God implores us to fix our eyes and mind on Jesus and not be of this world but to be transformed of it. And most of all that Jesus is coming soon, so we need to be ready. There is a strong analogy between Lot's wife chance of salvation and our NOW chance of salvation. [56]The Bible asserts that NOW is the time for salvation.

We're all in the same situation as Lot's wife!

Similar to the Lot's, we have a chance for salvation, we have been warned of the end of days that Jesus is coming back soon, that the only way to escape death is to follow Jesus and find refuge in Him. Yet we linger, like Lot's wife, because we are not ready to let go of worldly things and / or pleasures.

Jesus expressly warns us that we need to remember lot's wife because we are all in her situation. For a better summative review of our current situation, it is written:

---

[55]   Hebrews 12:2-3
[56]   2 Corinthians 6:2; Romans 13:11-14

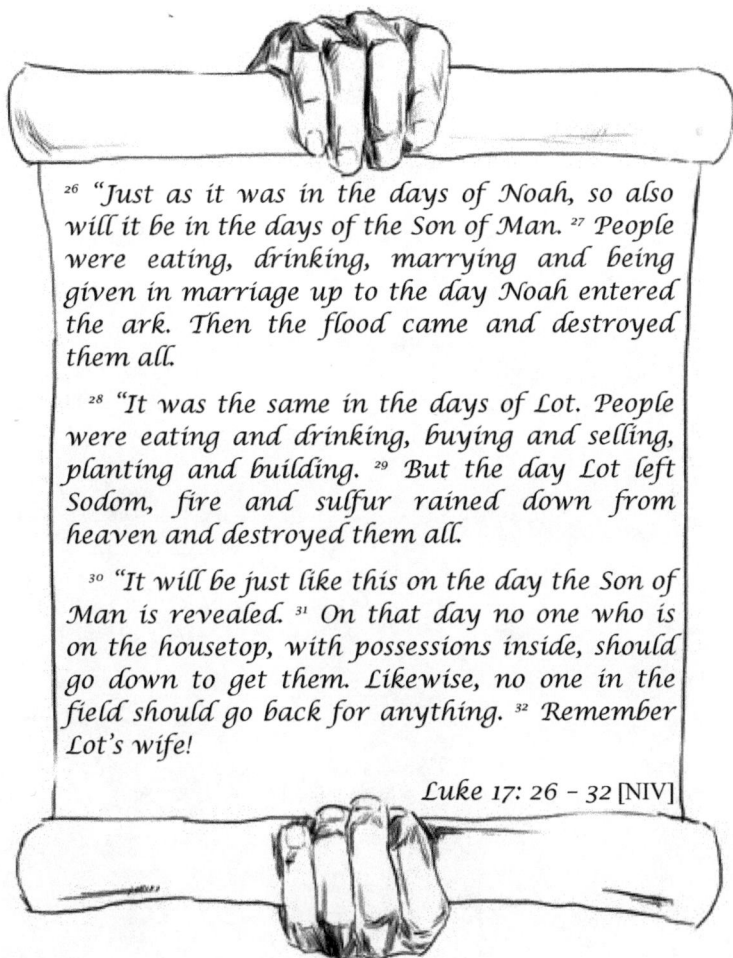

[26] "Just as it was in the days of Noah, so also will it be in the days of the Son of Man. [27] People were eating, drinking, marrying and being given in marriage up to the day Noah entered the ark. Then the flood came and destroyed them all.

[28] "It was the same in the days of Lot. People were eating and drinking, buying and selling, planting and building. [29] But the day Lot left Sodom, fire and sulfur rained down from heaven and destroyed them all.

[30] "It will be just like this on the day the Son of Man is revealed. [31] On that day no one who is on the housetop, with possessions inside, should go down to get them. Likewise, no one in the field should go back for anything. [32] Remember Lot's wife!

Luke 17: 26 – 32 [NIV]

(6): Mrs. Job

[JOB 1 and JOB 2: 1-10]

Mrs. Job was married to an every woman's dream kind of a man. In the land of Uz in the East, Mrs. Job lived a lavish life with her husband, Job, and their ten children; seven boys and three girls. Their sons were into entertaining a lot, as they took turns in hosting parties and they would always invite their sisters to come over, drink, and enjoy. They really enjoyed their parents' wealth.

Her husband on the other hand was quite the opposite of the kids. Knowing that the children were like 'party animals', he would pray for them with offerings to God, fearing that they might had cursed God during their drinking moments. He was a God-fearing man and was blessed with so much wealth, making him the richest man in the East. He owned 7000 sheep, 3000 camels, 5000 pairs of oxen, 5000 donkeys, and a large number of servants. By extrapolation into today's economic terms and considering time-value-for-money, the value of his wealth would probably still secure him a top spot in the *Forbes* list of the richest people in the world or the East.

In one of the meetings that God held with His angels, the devil was also present. When God happened to brag about the character of Mrs. Job's husband to the devil, the devil challenged God to take away His protection from the family.

The accusation was that Job was only a good person because God had provided everything for him and had blessed him a lot. The devil's contention was that, without God's protection, he would be able to harm the family, eventually causing Job to show his true colours by cursing God. As per the devil's request, God gave the devil a chance to prove his theory by allowing him to cause pain and suffering to Job.

What followed was a series of events that saw to Mrs. Job's life getting turned upside down. The wealth of her husband was all lost in a couple of minutes as each servant came to report how the different life stock were attacked and killed. The final blow for that day was when one other servant came to report that while the eldest son was hosting a party and as usual all her children were in the house enjoying themselves, a strong wind came blowing from the desert, bringing down the house and killing all their children inside.

We are not told of Mrs. Job's immediate reaction but that of her husband; he knelt down and started to worship God saying,

> "...We bring nothing at birth; we take nothing with us at death..." - Job 1:20 [CEV].

But the trouble was not over yet because, during the second round of attack, her husband developed very painful sores all over his body. This was still part of the devil's attack on him trying to make him curse God. But still, he did not! - He remained faithful to God.

On one of the days that followed, Job was seating outside on a heap of ashes to show God his sorrow. While scraping his sores with a broken piece of pottery, Mrs. Job asked him:

"Why do you still trust God? Why don't you curse Him and die?" - Job 2:9 [CEV].

But her husband rebuked her saying:

"Don't talk like a fool. If we accept blessings from God we must accept trouble as well." -Job 2:10 [CEV].

In all that happened, her husband never cursed God. The results were that God then blessed them again with double of what they had before.

Insight: The head and the body

In order to best understand the analysis of Mrs. Job and her family, let us first throw some factual light into the relationship between the physiological human head and body. Henceforth, the term 'head' will be meant to infer to the wider scope that is aligned to our prior references, including but not limited to ...

Jesus, husband, King, President, Priest, Pastor, etc. Similarly the term 'body' will be used with reference to the Church {bride}, Wife, Citizen(s) of a country, Congregation, and so on and so forth.

Power of the head

The head is in *total control* of the body, yet it cannot survive without the body. The main organ in the head is the brain, which controls the whole body; all the senses and decisions are controlled in the brain. As much as the body has all the other parts to sustain the head, the whole body is immobilized and *kaput* once the brain is dead.

After God created man, He was not completely satisfied. Once again we recall Him saying:

"It is *not good that the man should be alone; ...*" - Genesis 2:18 [KJV].

In this, we can infer that the head cannot function alone; so he created the body (a woman), that would support the head that was on the other hand created with everything in it.

Yes the head has the eyes, but can it move from one point to another to go and take what it sees? Yes the head has the ears, but can it run when danger bells start ringing? Yes the head has the mouth, but where can it keep and digest the meals it eats? In other words, the body plays a very significant role and needs to be well taken care of in order for the head to be able to achieve all its goals. This insight avers the popular claim that behind every successful man is a (strong) woman...!

Supremacy of the Head over the Body

Come to think of a person who, for whatsoever reason gets paralyzed from the neck to the feet. That person will most likely be confined to the bed. Nevertheless, he/she can still get whatsoever he/she wants done by assigning people to follow his/her commands. If for instance he wants to eat, bath, or change clothes, he will say what he wants and then the people he hired to work for or help him will attend to it. Similarly, such a person can make choices as to whatever he/she wants or be taken to wherever he/she wants to go even though unable to do it independently because of the paralyzed status of the body.

In the contrary, the case would be totally different for someone whose body would be well and free from any diseases or paralysis BUT have his/her head 'paralyzed' (brain dead). That person would be as good as dead; let alone getting what he/she wishes for, he/she cannot even make any wish or choice. As such, he/she remains absent and in most cases, such a person is occasionally released from this life through what doctors would prefer to call 'mercy killing' ... when doctors recommend the switching off of any life sustaining machinery hooked up to that person with the objective of *letting him/her to 'go'*.

It is very clear that it is the head that represents the life of a human being and should it be cut off or significantly destabilized, then one's life comes to an end at different levels, especially physiologically. Put in another way, important as the human body is, it definitely does not represent the life of a human being. So is the general co-relation between the 'head' and the 'body'.

LESSONS from Mrs. Job's life

It is easy to notice that there is very little that is explicitly said by Mrs. Job herself throughout the scriptures. Accordingly, we get to know her as a reflection through her husband's express communication and interaction with her in the biblical account of their life. As such, most of the lessons we can learn from her are derivatives from that reflection.

Lesson #1: The unity in marriage

Most people enter into a marriage covenant without fully understanding its implications. Not realizing that whether they believe it or not, they each die to their individual self the moment they are pronounce husband and wife, i.e. a new person is born; they become <u>one</u>.

It is misleading to view a marriage partner as an additional member in one's life because, considering what God says about marriage, the addition part fails to make any sense even from a mathematical perspective ... 1 person + 1 person = 2 persons, yet God says the answer is still 1 person. Therefore we can see that we could potentially have been using the wrong sign all along; instead of adding, we are supposed to multiply... 1 person x 1 person =1 person. At face value, take note that the addition sign (+) implies *combined efforts*, whereas the multiplication sign (x) implies *synergy*...!

Women need to be very careful when choosing the man to marry. It cannot just be about the butterflies in the tummy that you feel when seeing him or how good he looks and how romantic he is. The main thing to consider is how his relationship is with his Creator. If you are a child of God, the Holy Spirit will guide you in such a matter especially in giving you the gift of discernment where you will be able to tell when a fox in a sheep's skin has proposed to you. It does not matter how good that man may be in acting like God's child, your spirit will just reject him and it is best that you keep a safe distance from him. In the entire process, pray about it and ask God to order your steps.

The Bible has some examples of how a couple becomes one. We see it at the mention of [57]Cleopas who travelled with Jesus and travelled back to tell the disciples of their experience. The Bible says "two of them were travelling...". I have concluded that these were not two men travelling together but rather a couple. This conclusion is deciphered from the fact that only the name of one is given since the husband is the representative of the wife; by giving the husband's name, automatically the wife's name is given as they are one person.

Another example is when Apostle Paul, who was then Saul, met with Jesus in Damascus. Jesus said to him:

   "Saul, Saul why do you persecute me" - Acts 9:4 [NIV].

But you know that it was not Jesus in person that Saul persecuted but rather the believers of Jesus, yet Jesus said that he (Saul) was persecuting Him.

The explanation is straight forward - believers of Jesus are the church - the church is the bride of Jesus - the bride of Jesus is His body - as He is the head of the church and the church is

[57]   Luke 24

His body. As such, Saul was persecuting Jesus by way of persecuting His Church. As Christians we are one with Jesus, and that is why God sees us as righteous, i.e. as Jesus is our head and wholesome representative, then it means that righteous as He is, so are we in union with Him.

Adam too recognized the oneness of his wife, Eve, and himself. He acknowledged it when he said:

"This is now bone of my bones and flesh of my flesh; ..." - Genesis 2: 23[NIV].

From his statement you can tell that he really understood that Eve was not just his wife but that she was his body and the two were inseparable beings. He saw himself in her and I believe he also treated her as such.

Apostle Paul talks about the oneness in his letter to the Ephesians, teaching them to the effect that:

*"Men ought to love their wives just as they love their own bodies. A man who loves his wife loves himself. (People never hate their own bodies. Instead, they feed them and take care of them, just as Christ does the church; for we are members of his body.) As the scripture says, "For this reason a man will leave his father and mother and **unite with his wife and***

the two will become one." - Ephesians 5:28-31 [TEV]

Lesson #2: The man is the priest of his home (the head)

As the priest of the home, the man represents his family to God. If he is a bad an evil man, he represent his family as such and the same applies for a God-fearing man.

Just like a priest (or pastor) represents his congregation to God, that congregation gets to be corporately blessed when the priest does only what God tells him to do or say. More members become debt free, receive healing, prosper financially, give more, marriages thrive and multiply, and so forth. Why? The answer is simple and straight forward - God sees the church as he sees their representative. That is why it is for your own good that you go to a church where the only the *Word* of God is ministered and not otherwise. In that sense I identify clearly with what Kenneth Copeland coins as 'hooking-up'.

The reasoning here is that the priest as the leader carries with him seeds to plant into his congregation so that they may be fruitful. But the seeds he sows better be aligned to the *Word* of God because the type of seeds sown will determine the fruits that his/her church (the sowing ground) will bear.

The afore-going contention partly explains why some Christian congregations experience miraculous healings, and/or receive the gift of speaking in tongues and interpretations, and so on while others do not. If there are no such gifts of the spirit in a congregation, it means that the spiritual head is probably not sowing the right *Word* for such gifts to manifest. In essence, the sheep are blessed at the level of their shepherd's rootedness in the Word. In simple analogy, the health and wellbeing of a flock of sheep is a reflection of the shepherd's success in feeding and otherwise taking care of them.

One of the signs that a man is the priest in his home is that he carries the seeds of children in him and he has to plant them into his wife if he wants the fruits (children). But if he chooses not to plant in his wife the seeds he carries, that will result in them not bearing the fruits of children.

On a disclaimer note, I am not saying that God does not deal with us as individuals. Of course He does...! Just like in the agricultural sense of sowing seeds, the ground matters. The resultant outcomes have a very close correlation with the particular ground's fertility. Such is the case with seeds sown by the 'head' in ALL the other contexts such as the physiological, marital, political, and spiritual context. Nevertheless, the significance is highest at the sowing part of the process, hence the supremacy of the 'head'. To drive this point home, notice how almost irrelevant the ground's fertility becomes if no seeds are sown...!

In the case of Job's family, Mrs. Job's husband was a God-fearing man and we can see how God had put a hedge of protection around his wealth and children as a result of his honour to Him. As we read along the account, we get the idea that his children were not like him because of the way he used to always offer sacrifices to God on their behalf. This was based on his *fear* that they may have unintentionally cursed God while they were drunk in their partying sprees. So, even though the children were more interested in having fun and drinking themselves silly, God still kept them safe and well because of how their father represented them.

As alluded to earlier on, we are similarly righteous in God's eyes as Christians [58]through Jesus Christ. It is definitely not by our deeds. If it were for our deeds, then it would be very hard for us to be righteous. Instead, Jesus Christ is righteous, and is our representative in heaven. Therefore whenever God looks at Him, we automatically get the benefits of His righteousness.

---

[58]   2 Corinthians 5:21; Romans 3:22; Romans 5:19; I Corinthians 1:30

Whenever the devil accuses us before God, Jesus represents us as the church (His bride) and God sees us through Him.

In that same way then that Jesus is to us, the head of His church, so is a husband to his wife. The man therefore carries the responsibility of priesthood in his home, thereby representing the wife and the children.

Lesson #3: Supremacy of Husband over his Wife

In order to easily understand my argument in support of the Husband's supremacy, let us attempt to address a few inherent questions.

Question 1:

Why did Job's children die and not his wife?

When God gave Satan the green light to attack Job in the first round, He explicitly put a disclaimer:

"*...but don't harm Job.*" - Job 1:12 [CEV].

So the devil only had power over Job's possessions as God had removed His protective hand over them. And so we see Job losing all his belongings (including his children) except his wife, which makes perfect sense. His wife does not fall under the category of his possessions; his wife is part of himself, which now takes us to the second round of attack where God's hand of protection was removed from Job so that the devil could attack him.

Therefore answering the first question, the children died in the first round by virtue of falling under the umbrella of Job's possessions, yet the wife was not. She was an inseparable part of him under the marriage covenant ... the devil WAS AWARE OF THAT...!

Question 2:

Why did the devil only attack Job physically *(the body) when he had the chance to attack him both* physically **and** mentally?

Just like in the first round of attack, the devil attacked Job in a very thorough way in this second round too ... leaving no stone unturned...! [59]As we read about him having painful sores all over his body, his wife then suggests that he curse God and die. But we often miss the part that, suddenly, the wife talks like she has given up. She did not say anything when they lost their possessions, not even when all their 10 children died in one sweep. But when the attack got 'personal' in the second round of attack, she then spoke.

[59] Job 2:9

I am tempted to think that her proposition was partly from a point of realizing that the attack was on her as well. As a unit with the wife, Job was attacked *physically* and the wife was attacked *mentally*. In so doing, the devil knew that he was just attacking *one person*; the united *head* (Job) - *and* - *body* (his wife). Somehow having known his wife very well and upon hearing her recommendation that he should curse God, Job realized that it was unusual of his wife to speak in such a manner. In other words, it was outside her character. [60]That is why Job's response to his wife was not of calling her a *fool* but rather he asked to her not to talk *like-a-fool...*! In other Bible versions, Job is written to have said, "You are talking nonsense." Realize that Job was thereby asserting that she was not saying what he would expect of her but rather she was talking under the influence of a 'fool' in of her.

That instance of Job rebuking his wife reminds us of the instance when Jesus rebuked Peter, saying:

"Get thee behind me, Satan: ..." - Mark 8:33 [KJV].

Jesus had realized that, for a moment, the devil had possessed Peter and was speaking through him; and Peter himself was not the devil. Similarly as it was with Job's wife, Job realized that in

---

[60] Job 2:10

this particular instance she was not speaking out of her own accord. She must had momentarily been possessed by the devil who was thereby speaking through her. That explains why her requesting the husband to curse God was not making sense. In other words Job was saying ... 'it is unlike you to say that'.

If, for arguments sake, Mrs. Job's husband took her advice and cursed God, she too could have died in the second round of attack alongside her husband. She would have been as guilty as Job and judgment would have befallen both of them. This is because they would have cursed God as a unit, duly represented by Job.

In conclusion, through 'Job' as a single set of *Husband*-and-*Wife* in unity of marriage, the devil not only attacked Job *physically*, but also *mentally*...!

Question 3:

Why did judgement not befall Job's wife after wrongly advising her husband Job to curse God?

As already explained thus far, Jesus Christ (the head) and the Church (His Bride) are one body. Whenever God looks at Christ, He sees the Church and evaluates everything relating to the church by evaluating Christ. As such, born again Christians (the church) are righteous through Christ and not on their own account.

Similarly, Mr. Job (the husband and God's ordained head of his family) is the one that God's eyes were on; He saw Mrs. Job in the light of whatsoever her husband did or did not do, rather than on her own account. Her advice to her husband, bad as it was could only result into judgement if and only if the husband had taken heed of it. Put differently, if Job acted as per her advice, God would have judged both of them accordingly as one body.

It is mysterious to realize just how this observation resonates amicably with the account of what happened in the Garden of Eden. As you may recall, sin took effect only AFTER Adam ate the forbidden fruit, not just immediately after Eve's deception by the serpent / snake. It was only after Adam ate of the forbidden fruit that sin manifestation. Upon the manifestation of sin, they both realized that they were _naked_, which is in itself a symbol of _lack_.

In simplest terms, _naked_ in the context of Adam and Eve interpreted to their _lack_, which in a spiritual sense reflects their nakedness as the clothing of God's glory vanished. Notice that _sin_ apparently already _knew_ that Eve was just the body and it could not bear its fruit on them until the one who represented them, Adam, had fallen for the trick. Such was the drill with Mrs. Job and her husband, though the devil did not succeed this time around.

Lesson #4: Rewards of resisting the devil

The [61]Bible says that we should *submit* ourselves to God, resist the devil and he (the devil) will flee from us. And for our obedience to that *Word*, the reward is seeing the *Word* come true when the devil flees from us and the blessings that God then pours into our life.

In Job's family case, Job resisted the devil's temptation for them to curse God. After the devil had tried all his tempting tricks on them, he was left with no choice but to leave them alone. And as a reward, God then blessed them even more than he had already blessed before the whirls of temptation.

In our daily life today, we are faced with numerous temptations. They come in different sizes, shapes and colours. But the *Word* promises that we will never be tested more than we are capable of resisting. Therefore when we are going through testing times it would only make sense for us to start praising God, for two good reasons:

---

[61]   James 4:7

Firstly, we know that we are set up or rigged to win as nothing beyond our resistance can be used against us.

> *"There hath no temptation taken you but such as is common to man: but God is faithful, who will not suffer you to be tempted above that ye are able; but will with the temptation also make a way to escape, that ye may be able to bear it."* - 1 Corinthians 10:13 [KJV].

Secondly, we need praise God at the face of adversities and / or temptations because we know for sure that after the devil has exhausted himself in tempting us in the best way he knows how and we successfully resist him, blessings await us at the end of the temptation bout(s). In fact, more blessing than we had before the devil launched his attack on us...!

The reward is therefore two-folded; seeing the *Word* come true when the devil flees from us, and the blessings that God then pours into our lives. In Job's case they resisted the devil's temptation requiring them to curse God. The results were that the devil left them after trying all his tempting tricks on them. This was then followed by an overflow of blessings ... double of what they had before.

Lesson #5: **Fear** – Versus – **Grace**

A parallel insight as to why Job's children died

The way I see it, Job's children were unfortunately in a situation where their father was very sin-conscious. In lay-man terms, what that alludes to is that Job was *fearful*. YES, he was a good man who loved and believed in the Almighty God, BUT he had this thing called *fear* that was self-judgmental and law-enforced ... "I do good = I get good, and I do bad = I get bad " ... *karma* – as some people will prefer to call it.

God's grace is sufficient for all.

This fearfulness implies that Job was not fully aware of the complete measure of God's grace in his life, at-least not at that time. That unawareness created an environment for fear to flourish. I believe that this combination of ignorance and fear essentially constituted a small crack to the protection over his children. He was so fearful over their lives that he carried a 'responsibility' burden to the extent of trying to constantly apologize to God on their behalf ... "just in case they had sinned". And of all the rest of the good things he did, that FEAR was what the devil used to get to his children and more over try to steal Job's life with.

As parents we need to realize that loving our children has nothing to do with being worried about them. Most of us often mistake the element of *fear* with the definition of our *love* for them. In contrary, true love for them interprets to surrendering them fully to God, trusting Him that He is well able to author their testimony of life and to cover them till eternity ... not us, especially us mothers. We are vessels of His Love and our giving of that love to our children should never have to be from a fearful, worldly perspective whatsoever. We need to wake up to the truth that when we worry about them, which we too often do from an earthly frame of reference, we directly send a *VIP-Invitation* of harm to the devil and his gang.

Do we have to pray for our children?
YES we do, in <u>Faith</u> ... not in <u>Fear</u>...!

The fear of cursing God was Job's weakest link and the devil was very much aware of that. It is interesting to notice that even though it was not expressed as fear of him cursing God in this context but rather his fear of his children cursing God, that very indirect fear was what the enemy used to penetrate his family's circle.

This context is no different from today's context of parents and their children. It is quite common that a preacher will have one or more misbehaving child(ren) in the family. Being religious, these set of parents may care a lot about their children, be very strict in their style of upbringing, set very high standards or boundaries for them and so on. Then the outcomes end up being beyond what a psychologist can interpret or associate with a cause-effect relationship.

This seems to contradict society's face-value expectations whereby misbehaving children would normally be associated with a background of uncaring parents. In fact, and in numerous cases at that, some children raised by 'unbefitting' parents as judged by society's *casual-evaluation-system* end-up excelling and thriving in life.

As much as we may not be able to strictly stipulate what constitutes proper upbringing, the above contradictory instances defy any hard rules, psychology or theories. With all due considerations, Job's account gives us a simple insight into the way the Devil operates. When parents care too much about their children, it is most likely that they will tend to set rules, boundaries, targets, and expectations. They will try by all means to protect the children from the world. The more care they think they are exercising, the more and more the settings tend to become unreasonable. Unfortunately, and often without realizing, they step out of acting in love and drift into acting out of fear. For example being over-protective may seem like a noble act of love, yet that could be a reaction driven by fear ... a devil's deception.

To discern the difference between the two drivers of our actions, viz, *love*-versus-*fear*, we need remember that there is no fear in love. Worrying, especially about our children does not qualify to be any of *our business*. Our part as parents is actually made very simple; we are to carry and guide them to God by our words and being good examples. We are to surrender them to God, trusting and believing that he has them at the palm of His hands at all times and his grace is sufficient for them too.

With faith and trust in God as a remedy to fear, we can then live our lives under the guidance of love, i.e. guidance of God who is love, the very [62]love that casts out all fears. We need to remind ourselves constantly that whenever we to the contrary become afraid of any-*thing*, we effectively start walking away from love. By subconsciously choosing to be afraid, we gradually drift away from love and unlock one critical door that the devil uses in getting into our lives.

---

[62] (I John 4:18

Instead of surrendering his children to God, Job was always worried that his children would curse God unintentionally and then face the consequence of death. He obviously loved his children but he was not aware of the fact that as a parent, he was supposed to trust God's love for him and his seeds (children). By trusting the enemy's power to influence the children, he was actually endorsing the devil's capabilities at the expense of affirming God's supremacy in his life.

Lesson #6: Blasphemy

Why was it so critical that the entire story about Job squarely rested on the challenge of the devil towards making Job curse God...?

Right from the onset, we are told that God had bragged about the goodness of Job. It was then that Satan had challenged God that Job would curse Him if He gave him (Satan) the chance to torment him (Job). Why would Satan particularly choose and work so hard towards tempting Job to "curse God?" Why did he not try turning him into a murderer, thief, witch or whichever sinful thing you can think of? Why did the devil choose 'cursing God'? One thing is very clear though - that since God was saying Job was the 'best', the devil then wanted to turn him into the 'worst' ... possibly to be like him. The devil's mission was strategized at alienating Job from God!

[63]God loves us all so much. [64]He is rich in His grace and mercy. He can forgive us no matter what we do. Nevertheless, the Bible does have reference to a sin that refers to cursing God's Spirit. In the story of Job, this sin becomes a subject in two contexts: (1) where the devil is working so hard in the hope that Job would curse God, and (2) where Job was in constant fear that his own children would curse God, especially unaware of it while not sober-minded during their parties. In both contexts, the sin was not committed. In the first context, the devil failed in his attempt; Job expressly refused to curse God. Instead, he relentlessly blessed God irrespective of whatsoever was happening in his life.

In the second context and despite the children's death, commitment of the sin is not confirmed. We are only told of Job's fear and as you probably already know, what we fear *is not* necessarily what really *is*. In the mention of Job's fears we first read of him acting out of fear, whereby he was offering sacrifices after the parties for each child. The second time we read of his fears is when he says that all his fears have come true. This *implies* that he probably thought his children had

[63]   Romans 8:37-39; John 3:16; 1 John 4:9-12 ; John 13:34-35; Romans 5:8;Galatians 2:20; Psalm
        37:28; Proverbs 8:17 ; Deuteronomy 7:9 ; 1 John 3:1
[64]   Ephesians 1:7 & Ephesians 2:4

committed the sin during the party that they were having and as a result got punished by God through death. In my opinion, all I see in this latter context is Job simply acting and speaking out of *fear*. In any case, the "devil's challenge" was not about the children but Job himself.

As far as the sin of *blasphemy against the Holy Spirit* is concerned, I have neither sufficiently understood it to a level qualifying me to teach on it, nor have I yet received revelation on the matter. Therefore my input in that respect is hereby highly limited to what is written in the Bible and my scope is not scripturally or analytically exhaustive. Several theologians and other writers have explored the topic and reference thereto is hereby recommended. The scope of my input herein is very scanty and only necessitated by the event of Mrs. Job asking her husband to "curse God and die".

The Bible says that:

> *"If you see your brother or sister commit a sin that does not lead to death, you should pray to God, who will give them life. This applies to those whose sins do not lead to death. But there is sin which leads to death, and I do not say that you should pray to God about that. All wrongdoing is sin, but there is a sin which does not lead to death."* - 1 John 5:16 – 17 [TEV].

All the sins that we commit as human beings are to one another and to ourselves, but insulting God is different ... that is a sin towards God...! [65]The devil stands before God in heaven to accuse us of committing the sins that he deceives us to commit. However, Jesus is always relentlessly defending us, being our advocate. Consequently, God continually shows us mercy even when we actually deserve to be punished. That being the case, who then can defend us for such a sin when we choose to insult the very one who defends us?

"If you harm another person, God can help make things right between the two of you. But if you commit a crime against the LORD, no one can help you!" But the LORD had already decided to kill them. So he kept them from listening to their father. - I Samuel 2: 25 [TEV].

The quoted words were said by Eli the high priest addressing his sons after getting to hear how they were doing all sorts of sinful acts including having sex with prostitutes that worked at the entrance to the Tent of the LORD's presence.

And about this, God said:

"And I [now] announce to him that I will judge and punish his house forever for the iniquity of which he knew, for his sons were bringing a curse upon themselves [blaspheming God],

[65]   Revelation 12:10; Job 1:9-11

and he did not restrain them. Therefore I have sworn to the house of Eli that the iniquity of Eli's house shall not be atoned for or purged with sacrifice or offering forever." - I Samuel 3: 13-14 [Amp.].

Elsewhere in the Bible, Jesus said:

"Wherefore I say unto you, All manner of sin and blasphemy shall be forgiven unto men: but the blasphemy against the Holy Ghost shall not be forgiven unto men. And whosoever speaketh a word against the Son of man, it shall be forgiven him: but whosoever speaketh against the Holy Ghost, it shall not be forgiven him, neither in this world, neither in the world to come." - Matthew 12: 31-32 [KJV].

[66]We are further enlightened that at the end of days, the devil will come as a beast with seven heads. Written on each of those heads will be words that curse God. Clearly here we see that the devil saves his best act of disobedience, for the last show. This is the ultimate sin which he chooses to conclude with; cursing God will be his final blow in paving his way to hell.

Blasphemy in the Old and New Testament

Our ancestors knew the full weight of this sin. Throughout the Old and New Testaments we read that each time a person is accused of blasphemy, that person then had to be killed as the

[66] Revelations 13

law required. Since they knew just how serious this sin was (and still is), they would also falsely accuse good men with the intention of getting them killed.

And that is exactly how they got to crucify our Lord Jesus Christ; no one could find fault in Him and all that He did - so they decided to falsely accuse Him of blasphemy. They did the same to [67]Stephen, who was a preacher of the Gospel of good news. They could not find fault with him but they falsely accused him of blasphemy and as the law required, they stoned him to death.

Good enough for both Jesus and Stephen, they were being falsely accused. Jesus is seated at the right side of God in heaven and when Stephen died the sky opened up and he saw Jesus and commanded his spirit to Him. Unfortunately for the ones who really blasphemy God's Spirit, there seems to be no hope of them ever being in His presence in heaven.

Rejoice...!

Just like with Mr and Mrs. Job, the devil will try to make believers commit this sin; to *curse God*. It is by God's grace that we are born again, not by our ability or works. It is that very grace that protects our spirit from being corrupted by the devil. We are born again once and forever and whenever we

[67]   Acts 7:54-60

happen to sin, God does not keep a record of those sins, because He sees us through Jesus, who already died for all our sins.

We are to rejoice in that, once we are saved, the spirit of Christ dwells in us and that same spirit orders our steps in a manner that the devil cannot get us into blaspheming God. Job, God's servant in whom He was pleased, is a clear testimony to that; God's grace on him was sufficient to see to it that he did not curse Him.

How does the devil make us sin?

The devil's main mission is to trick us towards believing that God loves us no more. To counteract that, we should _always_ _remember_ that Jesus promised that there is nothing in this life and the next that will ever separate us from God's love...! When saying this, Jesus brings to light the things that the devil will use to try making you and I doubt God's love for us:

[68]_The devil's Seven (7) common tricks:_

1. _Tribulation_ (... misfortune, pain, calamity),

2. _Distress_ (... sorrow, grief, upset, anguish, worry, stress),

3. _Persecution_ (... maltreatment, suffering, harassment, torture),

4. _Famine_ (... want, starvation, deprivation, poverty, hunger,

---

[68]   Romans 8: 35

covet, shortage),

5. *Nakedness* (... defencelessness, helplessness, exposure),

6. *Peril* (... danger, vulnerability, death-trap),

7. *Sword* (... weapon, gossip) ... remember 'no weapon formed against us shall prosper'.

When all or any of these happen, the temptation that commonly comes is the deceptive feeling that God does not love us anymore. This is often accompanied by the after-taste thought that ... "if God still loves me, then this or that would not have happened to me in the first place...!"

Take *Famine* for instance; Hunger is one of the devil's favourite tricks. When Jesus was fasting, the devil tempted Him to worship him, an act that would have meant Jesus turning His back on God ... abandoning His faith in God the father.

Another hunger-related example is when [69]Esau was hungry and sold his birth-rite for a meal. The devil tempted him to abandon his first-born position; a position that is a symbol representing the one who is to inherit the father's blessings, one who stands in the line of ruling as the father (if the latter was a King) ... like us with the shared inheritance and ruling with Jesus when He returns for the millennium.

---

[69] Genesis 25: 19 – 34; Hebrews 12: 15-17

– JOB'S WIFE –

Remember too the Israelites:

> *"The people will wander through the land, discouraged and* <u>*hungry*</u>*. In their hunger and their anger they will* <u>*curse their*</u> <u>*king and their God*</u>*. They may look up the sky or stare at the ground, but they will* <u>*see nothing but trouble and darkness,*</u> <u>*terrifying darkness into which they are being driven*</u>*."* - Isaiah 8: 21-22 [TEV].

It is comforting to know that the devil has no power over us. The only powers the devil uses are limited to the authority that we give him in our lives. His works only revolves around tricking us into giving him that authority. For instance, notice how either the devil will cause [the *illusion* of] famine, or like in the above cases he will just take advantage of finding you in *hunger*.

God will definitely not always allow 'hunger' in your life but as a result of us stepping out of faith in God's *Word*, you may find yourself in a position of *lack* like in the case of Adam and Eve. The devil may then take advantage of that situation, which you will have attracted by your disbelieve; he will try and push you further to doubting God's love, hoping then that you may abandon your faith in God.

Despite the devil's efforts towards tricking us, we need rest assured that God's love for us is immeasurable and steadfast. Therefore we need put all our trust and hope in our LORD at all times regardless of whatsoever befalls us and/or our loved ones. May His grace be our beacon of strength and wisdom to survive devil's tricks in the face of our diverse humanly weaknesses.

Take note here that God used for good what the devil meant for evil towards Job, i.e. God used this opportunity to open Job's eyes to be conscious of His grace and not His law. He put him under the much better covenant of grace; one where you sow and reap a hundred fold. Before this we hear of Job's sons and his interest in them. Afterwards we hear of his daughters; the sons this time take a back seat. We hear of him leaving an inheritance for his daughters and his sons. We are even told of the daughters' names and not the sons. He now operates under grace ... girls then did not receive the father's inheritance as it was meant for the boys. But by grace, Job not only includes the girls but they are also the centre of his attention; they are the first to be mentioned concerning the inheritance. He learned a new thing that affected his whole life. He became richer, stopped stressing of his sons and treated his children from a grace perspective rather than a law-conscious perspective.

In conclusion, and despite all the devil's tricks, we have been re-assured that:

> "Yet in all these things we are more than conquerors through Him who loved us. For I am persuaded that neither death nor life, nor angels nor principalities nor powers, nor things present nor things to come, nor height nor depth, nor any other created thing, shall be able to separate us from the love of God which is in Christ Jesus our Lord." - Romans 8: 37-39 [NKJV].

Dear Mrs. Job

Possibly like many others, I too used to see you as an ungodly woman, one who just wished for her husband to 'curse God and die'.

Even though there is not much expressly said about you in the Bible, in a way you still manage to be revealed to us as we read about your husband, i.e. your true character of being a faithful woman of God in addition to being a loving and submissive wife.

For God to be able to use you into blessing Job with another set of 10 children, that alone convinces me that you had a long lasting youthful strength, which is only possessed by women who honour the lord by submitting to their husbands as the Word requires.

I feel honoured to have your true character revealed to me as I have learnt so much from your experience. Even though for a moment you lost your 'sanity', I wish you could give yourself a pat on the shoulder because you survived the attack through the bond and mutual understanding between you and your husband in your marriage. You must had been a great communicator with your husband for him to decipher when your advice could no longer make sense to him.

You made it through dear...BRAVO!!!

From your sister in Christ,

Pypie

(7): Samson's 1st Wife

[JUDGES 15: 1-16]

*S*amson's first wife was a Philistine woman that he had fallen in love with. Even before meeting her, the in-laws never approved of her simply because of being a Philistine. The disapproval did not only come from the fact that most Philistine women were prostitutes, but also because of their lack of faith in God.

Against all odds, Samson went ahead and asked for her hand in marriage. On the way to her father's house, Samson killed a lion with his bare hands. When he returned to her father's house a few weeks later to marry her, he passed by the spot where he had killed the lion and found honey in the dead lion's skeleton. So he ate some and gave some to his parents but he never told anyone of his encounter with the lion. He then went on to bet with the Philistine men at his wedding, giving them a riddle with a deadline of a week for them to come up with the answer. The riddle's answer was about the honey in the lion he had killed.

Despite being given reasonably sufficient time, none of the Philistine men could come up with the right answer. So they put Mrs. Samson under duress to find out the answer for them, threatening to kill her family if she failed to. Somehow she got him to tell her his then contextually biggest secret. When the

Philistine men gave him the right answer the following day, he just knew straight away that his new wife had betrayed him. As the bet was that the Philistine men would each give him a shirt and pair of trousers upon losing the bet, and vice versa if they won, he was obliged to get each of them the agreed set of shirt and pair of trousers.

In order to honour his obligation, he set out to their own town, killed 30 Philistine men, took the shirt and pair of trousers from each one of them and went back to his wife's home to give to his betting opponents. Then he took off heading back to his home alone and very angry. While he was gone, his (newly-wed) wife's father handed her over for marriage to one of the 30 men with whom Samson had had a bet.

Some days later when Samson's anger had abated, he went to see 'his wife' only to be refused entrance to her room by her father because she was now someone-else's wife. This really upset Samson even more, so much that he went to the Philistines' fields, and burnt all their crops. He accomplished this by way of tying up 300 foxes and setting them up on fire before driving them into the wheat fields.

When the Philistines found out why their crops were

destroyed, they went to Samson's wife's home and burnt it, killing her and all her family members.

LESSONS from Samson's first wife

Transition of Submission Authority

From the [70]Word of God, we learn that God not only wants us to *submit* to Him but also to any authority that he puts over us. It follows then that our parents become the first form of authority that we have ruling over our lives while they raise us from children-hood to adult-hood. Fathers remain the priests in the homes to their respective wives and children. Just as a priest wears a priesthood gown, so does the fathers even though we may not see the gowns with our naked eyes.

As tradition has it, the father hands his daughter over to the groom (the husband to be) when the daughter is getting married. As he hands over his daughter in the natural, spiritually he also hands over his priesthood gown to his son-in-law-to-be as they wed. From that moment onwards, the daughter *submits* to her husband as she did to her father. Spiritually, this is the man that then forever wears the gown that her father wore, thereby representing her father to her; the father whom she *submitted* to from childhood as the priest

---

[70]   Romans 13: 1-7; Hebrews 13: 17; Titus 3:1; 1 Peter 2: 13-25; Ephesians 5: 22; 6: 5-8

at her maternal home. In the context of submission, the marriage represents a seamless transition and effective transfer of authority.

Unlike in the physical sense, the father also remains with a gown that his own wife identifies with as her husband and so is the case with the other children. Therefore there is no contradiction or confusion. On the other hand, the gown that the married daughter now identifies with is the one that her new husband is wearing.

It is quite appalling to see what is happening today in the 'modern times' on the account of liberation movement for women whereby women are handing over their daughters as opposed to the fathers or uncles (if the father is dead). This practice needs to stop because as we know, spiritually the groom in these instances walks around with no gown of priesthood, which could only have been handed over by a male head.

God takes very seriously the leadership of a father to an unmarried woman on one hand, and the leadership of a husband to wife in marriage on the other. We see it in the [71]Bible that if a man makes a vow to the LORD or promises to

---

[71] Numbers 30:2

abstain from something, he has to keep it as He is the head of the man and there is no excuse for him to break his vow. Yet we further see a distinct change of expectations with regard to women. We are told that:

"When a young woman still living in her father's house makes a vow to give something to the LORD or promises to abstain from something, she must do everything that she vowed or promised <u>unless</u> her father raises an objection when he hears about it. But if

her father forbids her to fulfil the vow when he hears about it, she is not required to keep it. The LORD will forgive her because her father refused to let her keep it." - Numbers 30: 3-5 [TEV].

The woman here is excused from keeping the vow or promise in order to honour her father. We are further told that:

"If an unmarried woman makes a vow, whether deliberately or carelessly, or promises to abstain from something, and then marries, she must do everything that she vowed or promised unless her husband raises and objection when he hears about it. But if her husband forbids her to fulfil the vow when he hears about it, she is not required to keep it. The LORD will *forgive her."* - Numbers 30: 6-8 [TEV].

[72]The same applies to a married woman who may make a vow to God or promise to do something or abstain from something; that if her husband finds out about it and disapproves of it, then she is not required to keep the vow or promise in honour of her husband. Similarly the LORD will forgive her.

I'm sure you can now see that God sees a father and/or a husband as His representatives on earth. Once a woman gets married, she still has to honour her parents as the [73]Bible requires. However, her submission to the parents is subject to her husband's approval as her father already surrendered his power over her when he handed her over to her husband in marriage.

This latter predisposition is supposedly what Samson's first wife and her father were either ignorant of, or plainly naïve about; - what her father did was illegal even at the face of the judicial law *per se*. Even though Samson left angry without his bride, the fact remains that the father had already handed over the priesthood gown to him. In today's terms we would say he had already signed the *deal* and there was therefore no turning back. Samson left with the (virtual) signed contract and so the

---

[72] Numbers 30:10-12
[73] Exodus 20: 12; Deuteronomy 5: 10-16; Ephesians 6: 1-3

deal was still on; he still had the lady as his wife and that is why he expected to find his wife still waiting for him when he returned.

Samson's surprise was justifiable when he got to learn that his father-in-law had handed over his *bonafide* wife to another man. This simply implies that the second man had no authority over her because Samson still had the gown. When such a thing happens today, of which it does often happen that married people get married to other partners without ending the previous marriage(s), by law the succeeding marriage(s) is/are automatically rendered null and void. The preceding valid marriage prevails...!

As much as we love and honour our parents, we need be guided by what God says. Let us not perish because of our ignorance as I think that is what happened to Samson's wife (and father). Maybe she didn't know that her father had surrendered his power over her to Samson, and was therefore not bound to follow her father's leadership anymore but rather that of her husband. She was submissively required to wait for him till the day he decided to return. After all it was no surprise to her why he had left in the first place. And needless to say, she still owed him an apology for betraying him on their first day of marriage.

Bonus: Widows and Divorcees

Let us step aside from the context for a moment ... You might have been wondering about the chain of command in the case of a widow. Who does she have to *submit* to? The answer to this is given in the Bible to the effect that:

> "*A widow or a divorced woman must keep every vow she makes and every promise to abstain from something.*" – Numbers 30: 8 [TEV].

This implies that she is directly liable in her own individual capacity to the ultimate authority; the LORD.

Dear Mrs. Samson,

I do not want to be judgemental towards you because I do not know your side of the story. Yet still I cannot help it but wonder - what kind of a woman betrays her husband on their wedding day, and as if that is not crazy enough, goes on to marry one of the guys who had graced her husband's 'bachelors party'?

Sister you had THE guy! - he had God's anointing all over him, was from the right family, stronger than all your ex-boyfriends put together including the guy you betrayed him with.

Just in case you pull the card of submitting to your father, remember your father had already married you to Samson, and as such, Samson was your legitimate husband. Your father's assumption misled you into marrying someone else while your initial marriage was still valid. Your failure to submit to your husband, Samson, led to the death of so many people, including yourself and your father too.

Wishing you could have done better,

Pypie.

(8): Delilah

[JUDGES 16: 4-30]

...The Female Judas...!

*D*elilah was the second Philistine woman that Samson had fallen in love with. Since he had caused a lot of trouble for Philistines by killing them and destroying their crops when he was previously married to his first Philistine wife, the Philistines' leaders wanted him dead. So they offered Delilah money, which she would receive after informing them about the source of her husband's strength.

Delilah agreed to do as the Philistines' leaders had asked of her, but Samson would not tell her the truth. Every time Samson purported to tell her the source of his strength, she would later on tie him up while he was asleep and then scare him, pretending that the Philistines were attacking him. However, each time Samson would tear the ropes and jump free as if the ropes were mere strings. So Delilah kept on seeking for the true source of his strength. She nagged her husband so much that he finally gave in and told her that his strength came from his hair, which was in dreadlocks that he had never cut ever since he was born. This was because he was a *Nazarite*, a way of worshipping God that is very intense, and keeping hair uncut is one of the main stipulations to be observed.

As per the agreement with her leaders, Delilah went on to

disclose to them the source of Samson' strength. Later on when Samson was at her place, she got him to fall asleep on her lap and then she cut off his dreadlocks and tied him up with a rope. Samson lost all his strength and when the Philistines came, they captured him and poked his eyes out, making him blind. Then they took him to prison to do hard manual labour.

As time went by in the prison, his hair grew back and so did his supernatural strength. At some point in time, it came to be that the Philistines had a celebration gathering. They took Samson out of the prison, put him in front of everyone at the gathering, and started ridiculing him. It was then that Samson prayed to God saying:

"Sovereign LORD, please remember me; please God, give me my strength just once more, so that with this one blow I can get even with the Philistines for putting out my eyes." - Judges 16: 28 [TEV].

After praying he simply took hold of the two middle pillars supporting the building that they were in. Putting one hand on each pillar, he pushed against them and brought down the entire building. Alongside himself, he killed more Philistines in this bout than he had killed before during his life.

LESSONS from Delilah's life

Lesson #1: Character of a prostitute

Prostitution has been there since the beginning of sin; in the Old Testament, prostitutes would wait for their clients by the gates of the temple, just like they wait by the road today as more traffic generally means more people to seduce ... and so was the traffic by the temple gates.

It is all about money

The core mission of prostitution is to get money; it is a devil's way of making money, sacrificing one's being in order to earn something. I have not heard or come across prostitutes out there who render their services as charity. No...! – It is not for free; if you want a prostitute's service, you pay for it.

The contentions herein do not however include prostitution under duress, for instance the illegal sex trade whereby females and even males are kidnapped and forced into sex trade to the benefit of their respective kingpins. In that respect, I do hereby pay homage to organizations and activists working so hard and selflessly towards alleviating and remedying this societal vice.

As for voluntary prostitution, I can only imagine how hard it must be to sleep with different male strangers, leaving the prostitute feeling drained and hurt ... all but for money, and they still do it over and over again...!

It is a selfish act

I have heard people say, "Don't judge a prostitute because they do what they do just to feed their children..." It always sounds like they make prostitution to be a noble job. Of course I agree with the part of judgment that we are not to judge one another for whatsoever reasons and irrespective of the case. The judging should be left to God who is righteous to judge.

With the same yard-stick, our ineligibility to judge does not mean that we should speak well of evil deeds, one of them being prostitution. No matter how noble some people may make it seem to be, I still think it is a selfish act whereby the prostitute is all out about gaining at whatsoever cost. Literary speaking, I do not think that a prostitute cares that she is directly or indirectly destroying somebody's marriage, whether or not the money she is being given was meant to feed children, or pay their school fees, or pay for their health bills.

Further, I do not think she is concerned whether or not her services may give her 'client' and herself an incurable disease. I wonder if she realizes that she is seducing people to eternal death ... to sin against their own flesh. None of these things matter to a prostitute as long as she gets what she wants, as long as her needs are met. How it especially affects others is not in the list of her worries.

In my opinion, prostitution is basically motivated by the love of money and pride, two very dangerous ingredients to use in creating anything. The love of money blinds her into not realizing the amount of harm that she contributes into the lives of so many people including herself.

Pride on the other hand gives her all the reasons there can possibly be as to why she should do it. In most cases, the need to 'survive' is the reason given by most prostitutes and advocates of the practice. However, the truth of the matter is that pride shows a prostitute just how much lack she has and urges her to sell her body in order to meet her needs. Pride stands in her way of trusting God to provide for her and *whisper into her ears daily that He is with her.* Instead, pride whispers to her ears that there is no help out there unless she takes care of herself. Pride makes the situation to be all about her; how she is a victim of lack, poverty, and / or bad luck.

Prostitution is not only practiced in the context of women as seen selling their bodies in public places and back streets, but is also an attitude of the mind. Therefore we may also naively be practicing it as it may not be so obvious to everyone or anyone else but God.

In the case of Delilah who was brought up in a community where prostitution was practiced a lot, she must had learnt it from childhood. Gradually, it must had become normal practice in her frame of reference. That kind of stunt that she pulled on her husband, Samson, is one of a kind that can only be executed by a person with the character of a prostitute.

As you have already read in the previous sections about marriage, a man and his wife become one person when they marry. Therefore, when Delilah sold out her husband to the Philistine Kings, she was actually selling herself for money ... and that is what prostitution basically is. By selling her husband for money, she literary sold herself ignorantly thinking she was gaining something. She did not realize that she was actually harming herself and her act in itself constituted an act of prostitution.

Even today we have women who follow Delilah's foot-steps. In the news we sometime hear or read about wives who murder their husbands or hire hit-men to accomplish the *mission*, just so that they can claim the life insurance money, inherit their wealth, or with other hideous motive(s). We always wonder how a wife can get to do such an awful thing to her husband. Now that you know about the character of a prostitute, I guess you can now realize that such women are basically practicing prostitution at a different level ... They are simply prostitutes who give their services in the privacy of their own home with the husband as one or major 'client'.

I pray that there may be a repentance of prostitution in women so that we may live the life that God meant for us to live, that is, a life of nurturing, loving, supporting, encouraging, cheering on, and motivating our husbands. With such ability as women we cannot harm our husbands. We should always bear in mind that whatsoever we do unto our husbands, we actually do unto ourselves.

Lesson #2: The spirit of Judas Iscariot

I call it the spirit of Judas because, to this day we see people being controlled by the same spirit that controlled Judas. Judas walked with Jesus as His disciple, was with Him every step of the way as Jesus healed the sick, fed the hungry, brought the dead back to life, gave sight to the blind, and performed so many other miracles. Judas had the privilege of listening to His sermons and was even privileged to be with Him when he would explain the parables that He used as teaching tools.

Beyond any reasonable doubt, Judas was convinced of Jesus being a child of God but he was not convicted ... all the knowledge that he had about Jesus did not change him, so much that he got to be called a demon (one who has no hope of conviction).

[74]Judas felt so much remorse after he had betrayed the Lord, seeing how the Romans were persecuting an innocent man. [75]He therefore attempted to take the silver coins back to the Romans, which should have been the first step to his repentance. Instead of continuing with his initiative of repentance, he drowned himself into guilt and ended his life.

Similarly, Delilah was not married to any ordinary man and she knew it. She was married to a man of God. Even though the story of Samson and Delilah cover no more than three pages in the Bible, that does not mean they were married for a couple of days like it may seem. When we read their story, it is clear that Delilah also saw in numerous occasions the manifestation of God's Presence in her husband. Regardless, she remained unconvicted by that. She too was convinced of Samson's authenticity in being a child of God but somehow that too did not convict her.

---

[74]   Matthew 27: 3
[75]   Matthew 27: 3-5

I suppose Delilah must have felt some remorse when the Philistines came and not only arrested Samson but also assaulted him, gorging his eyes out. I do not think she was ever able to spend the money she got from them after realizing how much it cost him.

The spirit of Judas remains in our churches today, whereby you find people who have even been church goers all their lives. Some even get leadership positions, just like Judas had the 'treasurer' position in the ministry of Christ. Perhaps in the case of women, they become the preacher's wife and walk alongside a man of God just like Judas, seeing all the miracles and still remaining unconvicted.

The stories of Judas and Delilah are no different from our story today. As the church (us as Christians), we are the church of Jesus - disciples of Jesus -brides of Jesus ... we too have been walking with the Holy Spirit and have witnessed miraculous healings in the church, providence, forgiveness ... we have seen and experienced that, without a doubt, the *Holy Spirit* is from God and possesses supernatural power. But that knowledge has not convicted us all in church, because the spirit of Judas has infected so many people amongst us. In support of this contention, there are so many people for instance who religiously go to church but have not chosen to make Jesus their Lord and Saviour. They refuse to renounce the devil and all his works.

Camouflage of the Judas Spirit

It is almost impossible to tell in church if a person is under the influence of the Judas spirit or not; [76]look at how the disciples themselves could not tell that Jesus meant Judas when He said that one of them would betray Him. Instead, they stared at each other wondering individually if He meant them in particular. No one suspected Judas, and only after Peter had asked that John was informed by Jesus Himself. This means that you can never identify such a person unless the Holy Spirit reveals him to you. As you already probably know that John was the closest to Jesus, it is implicit that unless we have a close relationship with Jesus, we cannot know or identify the "demon" amongst us.

Unlike Judas who took his life away and Delilah who then disappeared from the pages of the Bible after betraying Samson, there is still hope for us today. Jesus died for all our sins and there is no need for us to feel condemned; [77]there is no condemnation in Christ Jesus. Unlike Judas, we must not let

---

[76]   Matthew 26: 17-30; Luke 22: 7-23; John 13
[77]   Romans 8: 1-39

guilt overpower us but rather be filled with the Holy Spirit and know that [78]we are loved and forgiven. We have been given a chance to live a new life by being born again. We have been given a chance to repent and realize the privileges bestowed upon us in walking with Christ Jesus our Shepherd, LORD and Saviour.

Dear Delilah,

Your husband came to you already bruised by his ex-wife and you were supposed to nurse and restore his broken heart. But no Delilah, not you...! - You decided to sell him out for some silver coins. Why Delilah...Why?

You strongly remind me of Judas Iscariot ... he also pulled a similar stunt on Jesus. Judas was said to be a demon right from the word go. Pardon me Delilah for I then wonder what you really were.

Very disappointed,

Pypie.

----

[78]   Romans 5: 8

(9): Potiphar's Wife

[Genesis 39]

A story is told of an Egyptian woman, married to the King's official by the name Potiphar. We also learn about a young man called Joseph who was sold to Potiphar as a slave by the Ishmaelites.

The Ishmaelites took Joseph to Egypt and sold him to Potiphar, the King's official in charge of the palace guard. As Potiphar's slave, Joseph lived with his master and the master's wife in their home in Egypt. Potiphar soon realized that Joseph was a blessed man, that whatsoever he touched turned into *gold*; that whatsoever he worked on became a success. So he liked Joseph and put him in-charge of his own house and all his property.

Joseph became Potiphar's personal assistant, aka PA in today's language. The only decision that Potiphar had to make was on what to eat and the rest was on Joseph. He is not only described to us as a man with God's favour but he is also said to have been very handsome. And because of his good looks, Potiphar's wife soon noticed him and became attracted to him.

Mrs. Potiphar went ahead and acted on her feelings by inviting Joseph to have sex with her. The response he got was unexpected to her because Joseph refused and said:

> *"My master isn't worried about anything in his house, because he has placed me in charge of everything he owns. No one in*

my master's house is more important than I am. The only
thing he hasn't given me is you, and that's because you are his
wife. I won't sin against God by doing such a terrible thing as
this." - Genesis 39: 8 - 9 [CEV].

Yeeeeap, the *slave* rejected her...! Joseph refused to take part in such an ungodly activity and clearly explained to her that he knew his place, explicitly declaring that he not only respected God but also his master. This guy was loyal to whom he served. But Mrs. Potiphar was unrelenting; she continued pursuing Joseph to a point where Joseph started avoiding her ... just how low can a woman go ... begging another man when she already had her own husband?

You may not always expect things to go your way.

One day Joseph was doing his work in Potiphar's house and it so happened that the other servants were not in the house. Mrs. Potiphar saw another opportunity to seduce Joseph, but he ran away from her, leaving her hanging onto his coat. At this point she must have realized that Joseph was never going to give in to her dodgy intentions. So she called one of her servants and lied that Joseph had tried to rape her but she screamed and he ran off, forgetting his coat behind. She even waited for her husband to come back from work to tell him the same lie and showed him the coat as evidence. Naturally, Potiphar was angry and sent Joseph to Prison.

LESSONS from Mrs. Potiphar's life

Lesson #1: Covetousness

According to the *Old Testament*, one of the [79]Commandments says -*'Thou shall not covet your neighbour's wife'*... (to women then: *'Thou shall not covet your neighbour's husband*).

Obviously your neighbour is not just the person who lives next door to your house. [80]When the Bible talks about your neighbour it refers to every other citizen of this world, making everyone on this earth your neighbour. The [81]Bible says that you must not want what they have; you should instead be grateful of what you already have.

I think we all do not have EVERYTHING we want, and every now and then we see other people having the very things that we long for. We see people driving the cars we want, living our dream lifestyle, having the children we have been hoping for, marrying the kind of man we wish we had, but still the Bible says ... do not desire to have those things if they are not yours.

What you appreciate appreciates in value.

[79]   Deuteronomy 5: 21; Exodus 20: 17
[80]   Luke 10: 25-37
[81]   1 Thessalonians 5: 18

In following the Bible's advice, we learn to *celebrate* other people's achievements instead of *envying* them. We learn to remain content with what we have and thank God for it - a great lesson of *gratitude*. That does not mean that we should not hope to have more or better things.

If only we can just learn to appreciate the 'few' good things we have, little as they may seem to be in comparison with what other people might be having, we will have so much peace in our hearts. If you appreciate your husband for instance, and as a sign of your appreciation you treat him like a king instead of envying other women's men who seem to be better than yours, chances are that you will start receiving the combination that you might have been eyeing on the other women's men, for example, royal treatment that we all like - he will treat you like his Queen.

Lesson #2: Coveting opens the door to temptations

The problem with envying other people's belongings is not only an attitude of being ungrateful. It also opens up the door to the devil to use us in numerous undesirable situations that can only lead us into *boiling water*. We are duly warned:

> *"Neither shalt thou desire thy neighbour's wife, neither shalt*

*thou covet thy neighbour's house, his field, or his manservant, or his maidservant, his ox, or his ass, or any **thing** that is thy neighbour's."* - Deuteronomy 5: 21 [KJV].

Temptation to steal

Since our eyes will constantly be glued onto our neighbour's belongings, our appetite for them will grow to a point where you cannot control it. And because we cannot afford to have those things at our own timing, yet our desires for them will be so great, we may find ourselves stealing from your neighbour.

That is partly what makes thieves steal. They constantly long for what other people have; other people's clothing, cars, furniture, money, and so forth. Instead of longing we should count our own blessings and give thanks to God for whatever He has provided us with.

Temptation to commit adultery

If you are forever wishing you could swap husbands with your neighbour, chances then are that if he would dare make a move on you, temptation would overpower you. That is why the [82]Bible says that wishing to commit adultery is the same as actually committing it. As in the case of Mrs. Potiphar, the only reason why she never slept with Joseph was because he

[82] Matthew 5: 27-28

refused.

As for Mrs. Potiphar, she had already fallen into the temptation. She wished for what was not hers; Joseph...! She thereby opened up all possible temptations to herself. Perhaps her husband was not as good looking as Joseph, or perhaps he didn't spend as much time at home as Joseph did. Whatsoever the case, he definitely was not as blessed as Joseph was and Mrs. Potiphar was not content with that. It is no wonder then that she was not only tempted to commit adultery but she also fell into the trap of sending an innocent man to jail.

Part 2

<u>**Women who submitted**</u>

Introduction

*J*ust like there are many women who failed the submission 'test', there are many women who did pass it in their particular contexts throughout the Bible. In this section we revisit some of them, uncover the circumstances surrounding their individual calls to *submit*, and map out the unique ways in which they passed the test. We similarly highlight the sometimes not-so-obvious lessons that we may learn from their submission and acknowledge their divine rewards for their exemplary choices of action.

We need however remember that the situations exemplified herein are again no different from our situations today. We too are often called upon to *submit* to God, our husbands, and other God-ordained authorities in our lives. It is not by force though. Nevertheless, the rewards are astonishingly beyond measure. You are hereby encouraged to relate the examples with your own past or current circumstances and/or experiences.

More importantly, I anticipate that this section will encourage us to be more conscious of the choices that we make in the course of our daily lives. The stakes are high, and so are the outcomes. It is my utmost hope that we will be filled with the hunger to be more receptive of God's nudging message, spiritual guidance, callings, and as a result become a blessing to many others through our very submission.

(1): Sarah

[Genesis 15 - 21]

- The anti-aging secret -

Beauty today is a multibillion dollars industry. A big focus of beauty is on appearances. Of my concern in the context of submission, so much money is spent by women on anti-aging creams and all sorts of portions that promise to slow down and reverse the irreversible ageing processes.

I have witnessed first-hand of how women can easily let a sales person(s) cleanup their account after a convincing marketing of an 'anti-aging' product. If you were to ask beauticians, skin specialists, cosmetologists or somatologists, most of them would tell you that 'facial treatments' are their most preferred treatments. The main reason would be that one can make lots of money in just an hour from after-service sale of products. This is unlike other treatments whereby the money one can make is heavily hinged on the treatment only. As beauticians, the main focus is on retail of the facial products while the treatments themselves mainly serve as a platform for forming relationship(s) with the client(s) and building trust.

Without sharing all the secrets in the beauty industry, allow me to reveal to you what your beautician will never ever tell you: "There is no cream in the whole world that can stop you from aging ... not one...!" The only thing the cream can do is to camouflage your aging process and/or signs. Unfortunately the world has its own way of working from *outward-in*, yet the Bible teaches us that things work best from *inwards-out*.

Beauty from *Outwards-In*

Countless women have been deceived that if they can put a particular cream on their skin, then it will penetrate into their skin cells and reverse and/or delay the aging process. It's all a Big Fat Lie my dear sisters; that is just one of the devil's ways of deceiving you into blowing-up your (current or future) children's inheritance.

Beauty from *Inwards-Out*

The Bible guides us into working in the opposite way from the world's system, i.e. *inwards-out*. Therefore if you want to slow down the aging process, it should start from within, and then the results will show on the outside. It is so simple, and it is not really a secret.

As we all probably know, <u>stress</u> speeds up the ageing process. We also know that stress builds-up from within. Therefore, it is implicit that we can deal better with the results (ageing) by dealing with the core contributory factors. Stress is basically a term that broadly refers to strain or overload that eventually leads to malfunctioning. It may be as a result of illness, emotional or psychological imbalance, physical injury, external pressures, dehydration, and stress-inducing lifestyle including insufficient sleep, smoking, doing drugs, alcohol abuse, poor diet, and so on. Whatsoever the form and/or source, the resultant effect is ageing.

We need look inside ourselves and find out what is stressing us so that we may deal with it. The results of stress free life will then inevitably reflect on our natural physical appearances.

Like an apple

Aging is like when an apple has worms inside; the worms savage on the apple from inside and eventually it start showing from the outside. Do you think it would make any sense to buy a cream or chemical that promises to camouflage the effect of rotting on the apple? It sounds crazy, doesn't it? Yet that is exactly what we do whenever we buy anti-aging products. It would make better sense to find something that can inoculate the apples against the attacks of the worms, a repellent of some sort that would make the worms find it impossible to attack the apple. Such a product would be priceless to an apples-farmer or horticulturalist, and definitely not the one that camouflages a rotten apple.

We learn in the Bible that, at some point, the Pharisees saw uncleanliness in an *outward-in* way - that when you eat (outwards action) certain foods, you become unclean (inside your soul). [83]To the contrast, Jesus showed them that the equation is different from the heavenly point of view. He emphasized that the equation is *inwards-out* when He said that what comes out of a man's mouth is what makes him unclean.

Sarah is well known for her submission, as well as her phenomenal graceful ageing. You cannot possibly talk about submission in marriage without talking about Sarah. She set the benchmark on 'Submission', and yet still, she cannot be left out when we talk about 'ageing gracefully.' In my humble understanding, and with all due respect to your own opinion, I do not see the two as separate traits of Sarah. What I see rather is that that very submission to her husband kept her from ageing.

Exercise

I wish you could do this possibly painful and yet awakening exercise for a moment: Compare two pictures; In Picture 1, visualize the wedding photo of a beautiful young lady - the lady (and Picture) could probably even be real - an actual character that you do already identify with - could even be you...! In

[83] Matthew 15:10-20

Picture 2, similarly visualize or actually assess how she (or you) looked like in five years' time or so.

How different are the two images?

If your character in the exercise (or you) has been married for longer than five years or so, chances are that the woman in Picture 1 and the one in Picture 2 are distinctively looking like two different people in terms of age. Do not be surprised if, just in case, the woman on Picture 2 looks like she is the mother of the one in Picture 1.

Sad a truth as it may be for most of us, it is also a wakeup call. In case there was a significant difference between your two Pictures, then it is most likely that something went out of balance / equilibrium with respect to submission.

It is quite common with us women to miss a piece (or more) of the submission puzzle somewhere along the line of our marriage life. As such, we need to trace our 'ageing issues' as far back as we can and try identifying the missing submission puzzle-piece(s). We then need dust it off and make an effort towards slotting it into its place in our marriage life. As you already understand, this applies not only to married women, but to all women. This is pivoted on the fact that every woman has an authority to *submit* to, be it your father, your husband, and/or the Almighty God.

It's very often easy to blame ageing on the 'ice cream', 'Chocolate', 'bag of chips', 'cakes' and the like ... let us just call these the *effigy-of-stress*. However, if you honestly look back you will discover that you have been bingeing on the ice cream or whatsoever because of this or that. You may even say it is "because of my husband," whom at that point you probably even wonder how he managed to convince you to marry him.

As women, it's no secret that we can stress just about anything and everything that our husbands do and/or do not do. And that frustration often leads us to our *effigy-of-stress*. In particular, I remember a time when I used to bake and eat more than necessary ... more like 'cooking up a storm' and 'eating up *the* storm' as well ... all in the name of, or as a means of steaming off stress. And hey, I should also mention that wine in so many cases would also do a much better job...! In a nut shell, the things that we do to *steam-off* stress are usually harmful to us - resultantly accelerating the aging process.

Royalty and Loyalty

Sarah normally referred to her husband Abraham as "lord". She not only gave him that title, but we can draw from that attitude that she also treated him as her lord.

Treating your husband as your Lord

As a Christian woman, the Lord you have most likely known so far is Jesus. Now tell me: Do you try to change Jesus to be like you? Do you try doing His job? Do you dishonour Him? Do you refuse His leadership? Of course not...! (...that is if you are a true Christian woman).

Just how funny then that when it comes to your husband, you do the exact opposite? - Changing, discrediting or challenging him can have the rude tendency of becoming your number one goal. As a tribute to the so called *liberation of women*, we now sometimes 'wear the pants' - sitting in the man's priesthood chair, trying to play both the father and mother role in our families.

We normally disrespect our husbands by what we do and/or say. For an example, men today have often been portrayed as *stupid*. In other cases they are simply targeted with all sorts of demeaning jokes, for instance revolving the observation that women can multi-task whereas men are, kind of, challenged in that respect. We call ourselves equals, thereby refusing to follow, or undermining their leadership. That is borne of a self-destructing attitude and perception, and it is not right.

We cannot call them Lord if we do not see them as we see the LORD. And that was Sarah's secret to her timeless beauty. She gave her husband his place of honour in her heart and that preserved her youth till her old age.

Sarah was able to see Abraham as Lord because she already had a LORD to liken him to; she was a Godly woman. Thus if you do not already know or have the LORD (Jesus) in your life, then you will have no one to liken your submission to your husband to.

Our LORD requires us to trust Him. He says that we should cast all our cares on Him and rest in knowing that He is in control of everything and wants only the best for us. Why not to let Him be our provider? The main point here is that as His bride, we are to walk around stress-free, trusting Him to take care of all our needs and concerns.

Similarly, just as we are meant to be stress-free brides of Christ, we are also meant to be stress free in our natural marriages. We are to remain stress-free wives, honouring our husbands through our submission and having faith in their God-given ability to take care of the family. That is the secret to our youthful looks.

Sarah's youthfulness

At the age of 90 years old, Sarah was able to carry a child for a full gestation period and to actually nurse him (Isaac). Pregnancy and taking care of a young child is very demanding especially for young mothers. And hey, it gets more challenging with age. Women over 40 years generally struggle to keep up with the demands of taking care of a toddler, let alone conceiving. I certainly cannot imagine anyone of this day and age being able to nurse a baby at 90 years of age. It really is virtually impossible today because we have made *submitting* such a horrible thing that seems to be a taboo to even discuss.

Today's women are barely making it to 75 years of age and are no match to Sarah who managed to nurse a child at 90. The few who do get to the 90s get there already so weak, with random aches and pains all over their bodies ... and then death becomes the only thing that they long for in order to end their *misery*. It is very clear then that the secret to preserving both the fresh beauty and strength that comes with youth starts with *submitting* to your husband. This is founded on living a holy life, which means making good lifestyle and matrimonial habits.

Keys to *Submitting* to your husband

Key #1: Having confidence in him

One of the best ways you can honour your husband is by having confidence in his ability to use his God-given ability to take care of his family (you and the children). This serves as good motivation for men to carry out their duties. Besides having the confidence, make it a point to let it show ... in your actions and communication.

That aside, you need to remember that he is a human being like you, and as such he will make mistakes every now and then just like you do. It is during such times that he needs your support the most. Remember therefore to boost his strength and motivate him to try again and do things right.

Key #2: Allow him his God-ordained leadership position

In *Genesis 3:16*, God said to the woman:

"*...and he shall rule over thee.*" – [KJV]

"*...yet you will be subject to him.*" – [TEV]

Be a truly liberated woman, liberated by Jesus Christ from oppression by the devil in your life. Exercise your freedom of having been set free from following what the world does (whenever under the devil's leadership). The world says that women must not let a man rule over them because they are equals, and that is the world's view on liberation for women. But as a Christian woman, you are blessed with the knowledge and understanding that the man was ordained by God to be the leader in his home. Further, you are blessed that you may see him as your *father* and as your priest.

On another platform, we do stand a chance to learn from well-brought up children. When they make plans of what they wish to do, they pass them by their father for his approval before they implement them. If he endorses the plan(s), well and good ... they go ahead to the implementation stage. On the contrary in cases where he disapproves of the plan(s), then the child has got to honour his father accordingly, trusting that the father knows best and that his opinion comes from a place of love, which in most cases is for the protection of the child. It would be so rebellious of the child to go ahead with his plan(s) even after the father's disapproval. Stunts such as pulling a long face towards the father or even whining as in an attempt of manipulating him to change his mind are just as bad.

The same applies at the decision-making platform between a husband and wife; the man has the last word, period! Just like in the case of a child, it would also be rebellious of a wife to implement ideas or plans that her husband disapproved of. It would even be worse if she tries to manipulate him just so that she may get her way, say for instance by pulling a long face or withholding 'certain pleasures' from him -you know what I mean...!

Key #3: Strive to be a holy woman

To be holy simply refers to making good lifestyle and matrimonial choices. In his second letter to Titus, Apostle Paul gives us a clear guide-line of how a woman can *live a holy life*. It points out the things she must do and the ones that she must not do. They include:

> ... Must not be slanderers (gossipers)
>
> ... Not to be slaves of wine
>
> ... Must teach what is good
>
> ... Love their husbands and children
>
> ... Self-controlled
>
> ... Pure
>
> ... Good housewives
>
> ... *Submit* to husbands

... (ALL THESE) so that no one will speak evil of the message that comes from God. - [Titus 2:3-5]

Elsewhere, in Apostle Paul's letter to Timothy, he makes some recommendation relating to church environment:

"I also want the woman to be modest and sensitive about their cloths and to dress properly: not with fancy hair styles or with gold ornaments or pearls or expensive dresses but with good deeds as it is proper for women who claim to be religious." – 1 Timothy 2: 9 [TEV].

Recap

"In the same way wives must submit to your husband ... You should not use outwards aids to make yourself beautiful, such as the way you do your hair, or the jewellery you put on, or the dresses you wear. Instead, your beauty should consist of your true inner self, the ageless beauty of a gentle and quiet spirit, which is of the greatest value in God's sight. For the devout women of the past who placed their hope in God used to make themselves beautiful by submitting to their husbands. Sarah was like that; she obeyed Abraham and called him her master. You are now her daughters if you do good and are not afraid of anything." - 1 Peter 3:1-6 [TEV].

(2): Shiphrah & Puah

[Exodus 1: 15 – 21]

*D*uring the days of captivity, Israelites were multiplying in numbers in the land of Egypt. They had settled there because Joseph who had earlier on been sold as a slave to an Egyptian officer (Potiphar) later on became prime minister of Egypt. Israelites were given permission to live in Egypt because of him as he had made the Egyptians' economy flourish as a result of his blessings from God.

After some time, Joseph died as well as his generation … all those who lived during his days. Then Egypt had a new King who either knew nothing, or plainly chose to ignore whatsoever he knew about Joseph. This king wanted nothing to do with the Israelites. He *feared* that they had multiplied so much that if there would be a war, the Israelites would take the enemy's side and help in destroying Egypt. So he made the Israelites slaves and made them do hard labour.

Despite his efforts, the Israelites continued to multiply. So he then ordered two midwives who used to help the Israelite women whenever delivering their babies to kill every male child that they delivered. They were ordered to only let the girls live. But because these midwives *feared God* more than they did the king, they decided not to follow the king's orders. As such, they let all the male children live as well.

When the king noticed what the midwives were doing, he asked them why they let the male new-borns live. As an excuse, they told him that it was because the Hebrew women had short labour. They went on to *explain* that by the time they arrived to deliver their babies, they would find them delivered already. Because of their submission, God blessed these midwives with children of their own.

LESSONS from Shiphrah and Puah's life

Lesson #1: *Submitting* the right way

These midwives knew that what the king wanted them to do was against God's way of life. So they did not disobey God by killing the children. The most impressing part is the way in which they handled the situation.

Even though the king was not a God-fearing man, they still gave him his respect and handled the situation in a very respectful manner, yet still without sinning. I believe that the King would have killed them if they had boasted to him that they we going to *submit* to God and not to him. They would have died and be replaced with other nurses who would be willing to follow the king's orders. Consequently, so many lives would have been lost including their own.

It took a lot of wisdom on their side to figure out a way of not killing the children (*submitting* to God) and yet at the same time not being disrespectful to the king (who also represents God in their lives as a God-ordained authority). They could have easily killed the infants to gain favour with the king. But it looks like they knew that the only favour they needed in their lives, and so do all of us, is from God. They honoured the divine hierarchy of submission by *submitting* to God first.

Lesson #2: Midwives dilemma

A message especially for nurses & midwives

This message goes especially to medical professionals and others entrusted with handling young lives. These are people faced with the *Shiphrah* and *Puah* challenge so often in their line of duty. In most of the USA (if not all) and South Africa for instance, abortion is a legalized medical procedure. From 12 years of age in South Africa particularly, a young woman can choose to either pay a private Doctor or go to a public hospital free of charge to get an abortion procedure performed on her.

Letting alone the fact that having an abortion is wrong and harmful to the woman's body, at times the nurses required to perform these abortions are born again Christians who only do them because they are in their line of duty. Just like the two midwives, nurses today also need to do whatever it takes for them not to take part in the murdering of innocent babies.

Of course I know that you need your job to support your family; so I'm not suggesting that you quit being a nurse, but just do everything in your power to avoid it and God will bless you dearly. Seek unto the LORD and He will give you the necessary wisdom as to how to *submit* to Him under your specific circumstances. Your job is to nurse people when they are not well and to properly receive human beings when arriving on planet earth. And hey, beware the devil is not happy about that…!

Nurses and doctors are like God's angels on earth; their job is to care for the human's physical life. That is an enormous reason as to why the devil is attacking them so much. Abortion's legalization does not mean that it is right in the eyes of God.

Performing an abortion would be *submitting* to the devil and guess what the result is…? - DEATH !!! In the contextual meaning of the *Law of Submission*, this refers to the DEATH of (1) an innocent being, (2) the doctor / nurse / midwife or whoever is performing the abortion, and (3) the mother of the child. These deaths are consequential and represented in the numerous forms of baggage that abortion comes with: wreckage or total write-off emotionally, physically, spiritually, psychologically and otherwise.

If you *submit* to God by not doing an abortion, the reward is the opposite of death, i.e. LIFE. In the simplest form, new born babies who will stand a chance to one day give birth to more human beings. The good thing about *submitting* to God is simply that the rewards go beyond measure; literary unfathomable - God blesses you in a way that nobody else can.

Take for instance the two midwives, *Shiphrah* and *Puah*; by not compromising their submission to God, He blessed them with their own children. That is an invaluable gift. Regardless of whatsoever earthly treasures that the King would have rewarded them with, he would never have been able to ever give them the priceless gift of LIFE; Children...!

Does this ring a bell? - In *submitting* to the Lord, they risked *their lives* by doing so, thereby sparing (sowing) *lives of the unborn babies* and in return (fruits) God gave them *lives*.

Lesson #3: Just how far will you go to keep your job?

The message does not only apply to medical professionals, but also to everyone else in their different work places regardless of whichever field one may be in. If at any point in time your superior(s) instruct you to do anything that is not aligned with God's *Word*, you do not have to follow their orders. On the same footing, you must not disrespect them.

In several of the different careers that we choose, there often is a requirement to market a lie to clients in order for the business to make large profits. We need constantly remind ourselves that we owe our clients the truth and trust that God will bless us with even more supporting clients.

I personally have experienced moment(s) of being given an order by my former bosses to sell a lie to my clients. As a therapist in the beauty industry, the more lies you tell to your clients the more money you can potentially take from them. This may be, for instance, by selling treatments and products that mostly don't do what they are purported or advertised to do.

At some point in my career I realized that I was taking off my Christian garment while at work and then putting it back on when going home. [84]This typical tendency is nothing different from the very thing that Jesus taught of as being impossible, viz, "serving two masters". So I then eventually made up my mind

[84]   Matthew 6:24; Luke 16:13

to tell my clients only the truth just like the two midwives' wisdom guided me. For instance I would sell products but tell my clients that they should not expect the products to perform miracles on their skin. For example, it would be pointless to do an expensive facial treatment, buy expensive facial products and then continue with the habit of huffing & puffing cigarettes ... there are no miracle products out there darling...!

The magic these clients were looking for was already within them, concealed in their ability and willingness to control their stress levels and living a healthy lifestyle. Notably, the skin conditions that they had were mostly as a result of stress and bad lifestyle choices like smoking, eating junk food, and not getting a good sleep. And needless to say, I miraculously still had my loyal clients and peace of mind.

How far have you gone in your career, just to secure a pay-cheque? Have you forgotten that God is the one who has power and authority higher than your boss as far as signing your pay-cheques is concerned?

Let us learn from these midwives and never take off our garment of Christianity when we get to work or in our other circles of life just for convenience, for example friendships, parenthood, community stewardships, parenthood and so on.

Let us pray for God's wisdom to guide us as we choose to *submit* to Him in our places of work and to guide us into *submitting* to our bosses without doing what is wrong in God's eyes. Just like these midwives, God will also bless us far beyond a 'promotion' that our bosses can ever be in a position to offer us.

(3): Abigail

[1 Samuel 25: 1 – 42]

*A*bigail was a beautiful woman, blessed with God's wisdom. She was a good wife and loved her husband unconditionally. I imagine that she must have also been fair and kind with her servants and above all, I trust that she had a prophetic insight.

Her husband was quite the opposite. He was mean and selfish; his name was *Nabal* - which means 'fool'. He came from the clan of Caleb and the town of Maon. He was a very wealthy man though, owning 3000 sheep and 1000 goats.

Before David was crowned King of Israel, he and his army had been in the wilderness at the same place where *Nabal's* men were herding his livestock. David's army protected *Nabal's* men and livestock from all sorts of danger in the wilderness and even helped them to look after the livestock at times.

Nabal at some point came visiting the location and had a feast as he saw to the shearing of his sheep. Then David heard about *Nabal's* visit and sent ten of his men to ask him to kindly give them whatsoever he had. He asked them to also tell *Nabal* about how they protected his men and looked after his livestock. But *Nabal* insulted David's men and sent them back empty handed.

When the soldiers informed David back in the wilderness of what had happened, he was so angry and planned to kill *Nabal*, his whole family and all his servants. So he took about 400 of his soldiers to go on the mission with him but while he was on his way, something else was happening back at *Nabal's* home. One of his servants informed Abigail of the story of how her husband ill-treated David's soldiers. Abigail quickly took 200 loaves of bread, 2 leather bags full of wine, 5 roasted sheep, 17Kg of roasted grain, a 100 bunches of raisins, and 200 cakes of dried figs. She loaded them on her donkey. She then told her servants to ride on ahead of her but did not inform her husband *Nabal* about her planned trip.

Along the way she met with David and his men. She threw herself on the ground apologizing on behalf of her husband for insulting David's men and she offered them the food. Then she begged David not to kill her family. She also prophesied to him that he would one day be king of Israel and would not want to carry the sin of murder in his hands. She asked David to please remember her when he becomes King.

David accepted her apology and went back with his men. When Abigail arrived back home, she found her husband enjoying his feast and well drunk. So she waited till the next day in order to tell him about how she saved them from David. When morning came the following day and *Nabal* had sobered up, Abigail told him everything about what had happened. He suffered a stroke, got completely paralysed, and died in 10 days' time.

When David heard of *Nabal's* death, he went and proposed love to Abigail. She agreed and went on to become his wife.

LESSON to learn from Abigail's life

Submitting when you are married to a 'fool'

Abigail was married to *Nabal,* whose name means fool; but that was no excuse for her not to *submit* to him. She *submitted* to him no matter what. She did her part of what she knew God's *Word* requires of a woman to do even though her husband did not do his part.

There are so many women married to men who do not do their part, and that is where we as women come in with our influential strong side. There is nothing comparable to a woman's influence. The good news is that we can use that influence in a positive way, especially towards leading our husbands to Jesus. If your man is really lost like in the case of Abigail, there is no need to stress about him and try to force salvation on to him. Instead, you are required to do your part even when it means *looking like* you are the one 'wearing the pants' at times; covering up for him, thereby salvaging him whenever he fails to take his position of priesthood. Remember that God is always watching and He will deal with him as He pleases.

Unfortunately for the ones like Abigail's husband who will are hard-hearted, he will be removed from you and God will give you a King to marry…Ha! Now please do not start praying for God to end your husband's life so that you can get your *prince charming*. Just keep doing your part and Know that God is in charge. Just like Abigail, God will take care of the rest if you continue doing your part of submission.

Always remember that if your husband is one who is hard to *submit* to because he does not do his part, (1) your submission may draw him closer to the Lord, and (2) if he chooses to continue hardening his heart, he draws judgment unto himself. Even though in marriage you are one body in God's eyes, automatically a 'foolish' husband separates himself from his wife spiritually by his actions and in no time the separation is manifested in the natural.

Separation - is a form of death; it is the main ingredient used for death. In other words, death would not be death without separation. Whenever death comes, so does separation. Therefore as death takes different forms, so does its twin ... separation. Take for instance death either in the physical or spiritual form. In either case, it is death and in due time it all manifests in the natural.

Therefore as a submissive woman, all you are called upon to do is heed your part and trust that God will evaluate the situation and do what He deems right accordingly. There will be peace in knowing that whether your husband accepts the LORD or chooses to harden his heart, the results will work out for good in the end. That alone should take away all the pressure we have of trying to change our husbands. God is the only one who can do that and He will force him - he will have a part to play also, which will be to accept and believe in Him, and take up his leadership role.

Recap

Likewise, wives, be subject to your own husbands, so that even if some do not obey the word, they may be won without a word by the conduct of their wives, when they see your respectful and pure conduct. - 1 Peter 3:1-2

(4) Rich woman of Shunem

[2 Kings 4: 8 – 37; 2 Kings 8]

*T*here was a lady in Shunem, a town that Prophet Elisha frequently visited. Every time the prophet went to the town, this lady would invite him for dinner at her home where she lived with her husband.

There came to a time when the lady requested from her husband that they build a room for the prophet on the roof of their house so that the prophet may use it whenever he visited the town. The husband approved and the room was built. One time when the prophet came again, he was presented with the room. Because he was so pleased, he sent his servant that he travelled with to the woman with the instruction to find out what she needs so that he could fulfil her needs. But the woman said she lacked nothing and had the security of her relatives living close by her home.

Thereafter the Prophet's servant enlightened him that the woman was short of a son and that her husband was already old. So the Prophet then called the lady of the house and prophesied to her that in the coming months she would have a son. That prophecy came to pass as the woman later on conceived and delivered a son. When the boy was about six years old and in the field where his father and servants were working, he complained of some pain. His father asked the servants to take him to his mother where he rested all morning on her lap. Unfortunately but by noon the boy passed away.

The lady immediately took her dead son to the room that they had built for the Prophet and locked him in. Then she went to her husband to ask for a donkey and one servant to travel with; to go and see the prophet. Even though the husband asked for the reasons motivating the journey especially on a day other than the Sabbath day, she chose not to tell him of the son's death and only reassured him to the effect that all was well.

Nearing the prophet's home, she was met by the prophet's servant. The servant had been asked by the prophet to meet her and find out if there were any problems concerning her family. Again she chose not to reveal the death of her son, affirming to the servant that all was well. It was only upon her arriving at the prophet's presence that she finally told him of the true reason of her visit. Even then, she still did not say that her son was dead. Instead, she said, [85]"Sir, I begged you not to get my hopes up, and I didn't even ask you for a son." From this response the prophet was able to draw his conclusions about her purpose of the visit.

When the prophet sent his servant to go heal the boy, the

---

[85]   2 Kings 4:28

woman promised she would not to let go of him (the prophet) until he went to heal the boy himself. So they set out to go all of them to attend to the issue. However, the prophet sent his assistant ahead with instructions of what to do. The servant did as his master had asked of him but unfortunately the boy remained dead. He only came back to life when the prophet himself went in to pray for him. So the lady got her son back.

Sometime later the prophet warned her of a famine that was to befall Israel, advising her to leave her house and only return after seven years. The woman respected the prophet's instructions and left her land. Seven years later when she returned, she was given back her land through the king's orders. Moreover, she was paid back money that had been made out of her land while she was away.

LESSONS from the Lady of Shumen

Lesson #1: Camp-Complaining

Complaining about all the things that have gone wrong in our lives seems like the one job we can do effortlessly as women ... no sweat...! ~ I bet you know what I am talking about; the stuff you talk about with your girlfriends when you have run out of stuff to gossip about ... the likes of 'Ohh, my husband this, and my husband that...', 'Ahh, your situation is better my friend, I have to deal with my husband, my teen kids plus my mother-in-law...' - We spend so much time complaining just about anything and everything to everyone instead of trusting God to take care of our plight in all circles of life. From my experiences, women seem to have a higher affinity for *camp-complaining*.

I believe we can borrow one phenomenal insight from this Lady of Shunem with regard to *camp-complaining*.

Her son died and she didn't even tell her husband. Instead of complaining, she focused on seeking a solution first, a solution founded on her faith in God...!

Oh how I marvel the character of this woman from Shunem...! As learnt from life experiences and later on from this lady, I always strive to avoid the habit of broadcasting my problems. This is regardless of whether a solution is under implementation or yet to be figured out. Before praying about them though, I have a habit of downloading them onto my husband. I go on and on sharing with him about whatever I feel or perceive not to be going well in my 'personal space'.

The journey of shifting from one way of doing things to another does not normally happen overnight, especially where long-lived habits are involved. Accordingly, there are times when I do keep discussion of the problems between us but from a *camp-complaining* platform. Unfortunately for him, even at times when I feel like he is not part of the problems, I still end-up aiming my canons into his directions, either targeting him on his own account, or on behalf of the situation…! And hey, I reckon I am most probably not the only one doing this. So sisters, I truly believe that borrowing a complete leaf from this lady may pay off.

As you may have already noticed in the afore-going personal account, I related to broadcasting of my problems only with respect to third parties. How about my husband? Can we justify the typical habit of placing him on the 'firing-line' or making him a virtual 'punching bag?' It is with these underlying questions in mind that I suggest we make reference to the Lady-of-Shunem's example; she set her eyes straight onto her source of everything and then chose to follow up the matter with that source, that is, God. In her pursuit of solution, she stayed focused on the source. How? She decided to go see and communicate her situation directly to God's servant, Elisha.

Remember it was through Elisha that she had gotten her blessings of the child to start with. It therefore makes perfect sense for her to go back to God (her source) through the same mediator / messenger path of communication. She was also favoured enough to discern that her husband and Gehazi were not necessarily part of the solution. By faith, she did not 'complain' to either of them – she only gave them an assurance and impression that all was well.

The power is in your words

There is so much power in the words we say, so much that I even doubt if we are capable of fully understanding that subject matter with our natural mind. Whosoever came up with the saying, 'sticks and stones may hurt me but words won't break my heart' must have said this out of ignorance. He /she had no clue of what words are capable of doing. This view-point is supported, and even makes more sense when we refer to what the Bible teaches:

> "The <u>tongue</u> has power of life and death..." - Proverbs 18: 21
> [NIV].
> "The Word of God is living and powerful..." - Hebrews 4: 12
> [NKJV].

This simply means that we inject life into our life whenever we speak the Word of God. In short, we are imperatively advised that:

...in your tongue (words)...choose life!!!

Words are the main ingredients used *to create something from nothing*. WORDS do become THINGS. You simply get what you say. Where does that leave you then if you spend so much time complaining (protesting / criticizing / grumbling / whining / nagging / moaning / nit-picking / fault-finding, and so on)? In complaining, do you realize then that this simply means you will just keep on getting more of the stuff that you are complaining about because you keep on creating it?

How?

As you keep saying it, it becomes some*thing*. As we said earlier on that words become *things*, your complaint takes the form of the very *thing* that you are saying / voicing out. Simply put, if you talk about bananas you get bananas ... not apples! Just like when God said, "Light be", His WORDS took form and there was light ... not darkness or something else! Since your words take form based on what you *say*, it is no rocket-science to see that whenever you complain you only *say* what you do not like. To your pretended surprise then, what you keep complaining about will inevitably manifest because of your ingenious art of creating it.

Notice how you can almost always sense the energy engraved in someone's words. Consider for instance the tone of words voiced out in anger versus words uttered with the intention of communicating love. I guess that is partly why there is a saying to the effect that ... 'If you have nothing good to say, do not say anything at all'.

Lesson #2: Words are seeds

In the book of *Genesis*, God is introduced to us as one who uses *words* to make *things*, and then as a gardener when he plants the Garden of Eden. This evidence points out to me that these steps follow each other for a reason. I have learnt that words are also seeds. As I can only imagine, He *planted* His words in that garden, which then took form and grew to produce fruits.

At the back of my mind I still remember that we were made in His likeness. So we similarly can use *words* as *seeds*. We sow them and they eventually become things that are to us the harvest.

Each of us consistently possess two bags of seeds (or words); on your right there is the bag of faithful seeds and on your left the bag of faithless seeds. Each day we are to choose which one of the bags to use. This is where Jesus then advises us to choose from the faithful bag so that we will have a good harvest.

So every day I wake up consciously knowing that I carry two bags of seeds with me wherever I go. Then I pray that God may shower me with His wisdom, wisdom to guide me on when, where, and how to sow my seeds and to always choose from the good bag.

At another level of understanding, it means that the bags of seeds I carry along are simply all the words in me. I pray that God may guide me on *what to say* under different circumstances and to different people. The knowledge that the words I speak become *things* makes me seek God more and more in the issue of opening my mouth to talk. I strive to make sure that whatsoever I say is aligned with His *Word*. It is my goal to always speak in God's language; Faith. This is all in the hope that I may spend my day(s) sowing words of faith that will produce only good fruits.

What not to say

In the same way as *faith-filled* words work, so does *faith-less* ones. But bear in mind that words with no faith in them are not from God as I mentioned that faith is God's language. It is like receiving a letter written in Chinese, for instance, and claiming that you got it from me or someone else, knowing very well that I or the other person neither understands nor speaks or writes in Chinese. That is just as good as impossible unless you received an interpreted version of the original letter, which would in any case be written in a mother-tongue or common language of reference. Faith is God's common *spiritual* language of reference.

Accordingly, *faithless seeds* or *faithless words*, which are the same as doubtful words then are from the devil. We ought to pray that we receive God's wisdom to always pick the faithful bag of seeds and to let the doubtful bag remain sealed. Figuratively speaking, we may hope that in due time the faithless seeds will reach their expiry date such that even if we mistakenly sow them, they will not bear any fruits. That way, and through God's Grace, we will always heed to the His advice: [86]'...choose life'.

Lesson #3: Offering the sacrifice of praise to God (even in times of trouble)

If we choose to complain about whatsoever situation we may find ourselves in, we should at least do so knowing very well

[86] Deuteronomy 30:19

that we are planting seeds of destruction that will grow up to produce *deadly* fruits.

The Lady from Shunem knew the power of words. She set a perfect example for us on how to deal with especially difficult situations. She exemplifies so much wisdom with her seemingly 'worst case scenario' situation, quite differently from what common intuition would tend to dictate. She chose to speak words of faith in a situation where most of us would surely complain, either directly or indirectly, consciously or sub-consciously.

When her husband asked her why she was going to see the prophet yet it was not a religious day, he was in other words saying 'what is so *wrong* that you must go and see a prophet on a non-religious day?' By only telling him not to worry, it displays her divine wisdom in knowing where to plant her seed. Telling her worrisome husband about the death of their son would have done her no good. Instead, it would have risked her being infected by his worry and thereby possibly pulling her away from faith. That would have been a chance for the devil to sow a seed of doubt!

Notice that she did the same to Gehazi, Elisha's assistant. When he also asked her in *many words* what was *wrong*, she responded:

   ..."*Everything is fine*" - 2 Kings 4: 26 [CEV].

It was only when she got to Elisha (a man who represented God to her), that he spoke of her situation in faith. She caught Elijah by the feet and declared her ground of faith, affirming the origin of her son, and her expectation that he should sort out the situation.

As sure as the sun rises from the East, there will always be open chances coming our way to complain whenever we are faced with, or going through difficult times. Let us all remember the lady of Shunem and say all is well whenever people try talking us into complaining. For those close to us like our husbands with whom we may be going through the hard times, let us take our positions of being helpers, telling them not to worry, reminding them our true source of whatsoever we have and from whom all our help comes. Then we go down on our knees like the lady of Shunem and tell God about the situation and hang on to him in faith. Just as the lady of Shunem got her son back, so will we get back whatsoever the devil may have tried stealing away from our families.

It is worth noting that when Elisha sent his assistant, Gehazi, the Lady of Shunem still hang on to him. She was not moved by

Elisha's idea of sending the assistant. She never let go until Elisha himself (her contextual God's representative) moved. She not only praised God but also averred her acknowledgement of Elisha as God's servant when she said:

"… As the LORD liveth, and as thy soul liveth, I will not leave thee…" - 2 Kings 4: 30 [KJV].

It is only sensible then for us to also praise God during our times of trouble as she did. Similarly we also need acknowledge God's servants, who in our particular circles may be our Priests, Pastors, Prophets, Rabbis, and so on. Nevertheless, we need always bear in mind that as much as they are God-ordained representatives, our faith rests not in them but in God who ordained them. They serve God and are not His replacements. We should respect and see them as His representatives, always knowing that we are all God's servants with different callings (Gifts) and all the help we will ever need only comes from God Himself.

The Lady of Shunem seems to have figured out the different levels of authority. When she saw Elisha sending his servant, she persisted, waiting only for him to move. This is sure testimony that her faith made all the difference. She wanted to leave no room for doubt. As such she solely counted on Elisha

himself, through whom she had absolute faith in God's power
and ability to restore her situation regarding her son's death.

(5) Woman from Zarephath

[1 Kings 17: 8-24; Luke 4: 26]

*9*n the town of Zarephath there lived a widow with her son. At that time there was a drought in their land. Looking at her food storage one day she realized that her food reserves had come to the 'end of the road'. She therefore set out to make plans of cooking her last meal. In her frame of thoughts, she would then have to starve to death together with her son.

So she went out to collect fire wood for preparation of the last meal. On her way back home, however, a man approached her. He was Elijah, God's prophet sent by God to go and be fed by this widow. He asked her to offer him some water to drink. As she willingly went on to fetch him the water, he added onto his *tab* that she must please prepare a meal for him. Because of her situation, she explained to the man that she would love to but she had run out of food. She explained to him:

> *"By the living LORD your God I swear that I haven't got any bread. All I have is a handful of flour in a bowl and a drop of olive-oil in a jar. I came here to gather some firewood to take back home and prepare what little I have for my son and me. That will be our last meal, and then we will starve to death."* - 1 Kings 17: 12 [TEV].

But the man reiterated his request, declaring that she should not worry, further suggesting that she should actually first prepare and serve him a small loaf and then prepare the rest for herself and her son. He went on to proclaim God's message to her, saying:

> ... "The bowl will not run out of flour or the jar run out of oil before the day that I, the LORD, send rain" - 1 Kings 17: 14 [TEV].

As hard to believe as it would be to anyone in the Lady's situation, she obeyed the man. She obeyed an unexpected visitor...! Does that sound to you like gambling? In obedience, she did as he asked and indeed, she never ran out of food; God supernaturally supplied her with food as long as the drought was on. She was having a totally different experience of endless food supply:

> "As the LORD had promised through Elijah, the bowl did not run out of flour nor did the jar run out of oil." - 1 Kings 17: 16 [TEV].

LESSONS to be learned

Lesson #1: Tithing

Somehow the story of this woman takes me back to *tithing*. Notice how Elijah asked her to give him what she had, clarifying that in so doing she should prepare for him first and then prepare the rest for herself and her son. It is the same way that we are required to give tithes to God; we are meant to give him first and then use the remainder for our needs and wants.

In the [87]*Old Testament*, there are several references where tithing was pegged at 10% of the subject matter. In cases where people were farming as a means of making a living, the requirement was to offer the first fruits of their harvest. With respect to their livestock, the first born male animals had to be offered as a sacrifice. In all these cases, God is simply saying to the people, 'Make me your first priority; give to me first and then watch me bless you.' Jesus said:

"But rather seek ye the kingdom of God; and all these things shall be added unto you." - Luke 12: 31 [KJV].

The rest of the things to follow are obviously blessings from God after we have put Him first in our lives. And what better way can that be other than by giving Him a portion of our treasure? As the [88]Bible says, "For where your treasure is, there will your heart be also." So by tithing we are constantly giving our hearts out to God, which means we are worshipping Him and coming to Him in the only language He understands; faith.

---

[87]   Numbers. 18:20-26; 1 Sam. 8:14-17; Genesis 14:20; Deut. 12:6-7; 14:22-23
[88]   Matthew 6:21 [KJV]

If we give first to Him, the question that is often provoked in us then becomes - "What if the remainder will not be enough for me?" That is why tithing takes (1) an attitude of obedience; saying that since God said we should tithe, then we will even though it just may not seem to add up for us in the natural, (2) having faith that since He said that what will follow are blessings, then it shall all come to pass even though we do not see or know how, where, and when. In other words, we then just choose to believe it only because God said it, and (3) appreciating that tithing is a tool of praise and worship in the sense that when we tithe, we in substance honour God in thanksgiving and love.

The lady from Zarephath must have gone through the same experience as we go through whenever we have to tithe. Do you think it would have been any easier if she was being asked for food at a time when she had plenty? Most likely yes, but then it would definitely not be as much an exercise of faith in so doing. It was perfect timing that she was at a point where she had just one meal left, putting her in a position of choosing either *common sense* or *obedience*.

Common sense would have said - "Hey, there is famine in the land and everybody is starving to death and this *guy* is just out here to con me off my last meal. The worst part is that he is not just asking me to leave some of the meal for him but rather he wants me to serve him first. No ways...! – this cannot be a man of God because God is a giver and not a taker. And in any case, if he is really sent by God, then God would have known that I need to be given food in the first place ... not the other way round!"

If the lady went with the drift of what *common sense* was probably saying, then her story would have been very different. We would most likely be reading of how she and her son died after their last meal while Elijah got provided for in another way by God. But instead, we now read about how their lives were superfluously blessed in a time of famine. This message rhymes with the feeling that, 'in hanging onto whatsoever we have, we lose it; and in giving it away, we get so much more of it in several folds'. Does that sound familiar? Have you had such an experience? It may be easier for some readers to relate this to the commonly known *law of attraction*.

As for this Lady from Zarephath, she went for the voice of faith which says:

> "...*Put me to the test and you will see that I will open the windows of heaven and pour out on you in abundance all kinds*

of good things. I will not let insects destroy your crops and your grapevines will be loaded with grapes. Then the people of all nations will call you happy, because your land will be a good place to live in" - Malachi 3:10-12 [TEV].

Let us learn from this woman that our circumstances should not overshadow the *Word* of God. We need to continue *obeying* God and having faith in Him even when it seems like what His *Word* requires us to do makes no sense. The same *Word* that came to this woman is the same *Word* that comes to us today and as she handled the situation with *obedience* and faith, we too need to follow in her footsteps. As the [89]Bible says, God is not a respecter of man and therefore He can do for us too what He did for her if we also obey Him.

Tithing interprets to submission

Tithing pleases God, because it makes us to operate in faith and *obedience* to God. He then blesses us as He promises in His *Word*. On the other hand, *failure to tithe* does exactly the opposite; it opens up the window of curses. As tithing prompts God's actions, failure to tithe equally prompts the curse actions.

We see that clearly in the story of Abel and Cain who were Adam and Eve's children. Abel was a shepherd and he took the

[89] Acts 10:34-35; Romans 2: 9-11

first born lamb, killed it and offered the best part of it as an offering to God. This was absolute *submission* and it pleased God a lot. [90]His brother Cain, who was a farmer, offered his *late harvest* and consequently God was not pleased with it.

Note that Abel not only gave the best parts of the lamb but it was the first born male.

> *"Honour the LORD by making Him an offering from the best of all that your land produces. If you do, your barns will be filled with grains, and you will have too much wine to be able to store it all."* - Proverbs 3: 9-10 [TEV].

Cain could also have pleased God if he had offered the *first fruits* from his harvest, thereby putting God first. His failure to do so (failure to *submit*) became a window for devil's attack with the end results of him killing his own and then only brother, Abel.

Lesson #2: Seed Sowing

God has given to every one of us human beings enough seeds to sow in order for us to experience an abundance of possession and spiritual blessings. The reason why most never experience this is not because God is not faithful to His *Word*, but because they have little or no faith in God's *Words*. As such,

[90] Genesis 4: 2-7

they consequently hold back in sowing their God given seeds in *fear* of the possibility of them not germinating and bringing forth fruits.

Always remember that God made us all in His own image and likeness. Therefore in so many ways we take after our creator and Father, for instance as carriers of a variety of seeds to sow. Seed sowing takes us back to God's original plan for mankind to enter into His rest; His finished works. The last in God's creation were human beings and the next day was a day of rest from His works. In other words, after humans were created, there was no more creation that followed. From another perspective, God had made provisions for everything by the time He created us human beings. Further, [91]God blessed us to multiply, be fruitful, fill the earth ... and this is a blessing of reproduction.

Reproduction in the literal sense refers to the process or action of making a copy of something. For the continuation of life, we are to receive God's first blessing upon us. You see here that God created everything and then created people in His likeness, who for survival purposes will have to copy Him. Figuratively speaking, He provided all the originals and our part is to keep the 'copying machine' running.

[91] Genesis 1: 28

Mother-Nature affirms the afore-going premise. Take note that fruits have seeds in their core. Imperatively then, remember to not to eat the whole fruit when enjoying yours ... spare the seed! Beware that if you eat the seed too, you will be cutting off future supply. Therefore simply enjoy your fruits but take out the seeds and re-plant them.

As for the woman of Zarephath, a measure of faith must had been poured into her in order for her to heed Elijah's request under her particular circumstances of scarcity. Remember that [92]faith comes by hearing and hearing by the *Word* of God. She now exercised this faith that she had received; for the first time in her life, she trusted God for her supply and not her own ability to search for food or to ration it.

What her eyes were opened to in order to see God's provision was that her last meal was like one last fruit that she had. As such, she was made to see that there still was hope for tomorrow because even though the *fruit* may had been one and even had to share it with her son, in it there was a *seed* that when planted in *God's ministry* would grow into a *tree* that would bring forth numerous *fruits*.

So she baked a small loaf first for Elijah, which was intrinsically a form of planting her *seed* under God's guidance. Take note that

[92] Romans 10:17

Elijah asked for just a small loaf - *seeds* are naturally small, yet their produce is incomparable to them in size and number. Further, the fruits borne of a seed take the form and genealogy of the fruit from which the seed came. Accordingly, take note of how her *fruits* constituted the continued supply of that very thing that she sowed; she never ran out of food right through the time of famine.

Considering fruits in a literal sense, I trust that this concept is not hard to understand when you are having a full supply of fruits. You simply eat some, give out some to others, and definitely the wise-few will plant some of the seeds to maintain the supply. In times of scarcity, however, the terms of reference are inclined to change. Think, for instance, of a period of famine when the supply is scarce. The natural feeling is to hang on to the fruit as much as you can and not to give or share with anyone.

In particular, let us consider a peasant farmer with a small bag of grains of maize and / or beans. These very grains can either be eaten or sowed, yet there is no distinction between their "seed" and the "food" nature. Irrespective of the circumstances, the owner has to have the wisdom on what proportion to eat and what proportion to sow. As food for thought, notice here the inherent *freedom of choice*.

The message is very clear, that whatsoever one has and no matter how small or insignificant it may seem to be, is a type of seed-containing fruit. These fruits include, amongst many others, food, innovative ideas, memories, property, a smile, a prayer, money, kindness, friendship, encouragement, a helping hand, fairness, time, God's *Word*, motivation, thoughts, care, love, knowledge, and justice. In as much as fruits come in different sizes and forms, it is for us to know that within every fruit bestowed upon us is a seed that is meant to be sowed in order for us to have fruits again tomorrow.

With the afore-going understanding and now looking back at the woman of Zarephath, this woman was in a time of famine with her last meal. You can imagine she must had done all she could to stretch the available limited supply by carefully rationing it between her and her son, as well as from meal to meal and from day to day. Punctually as ever always, God came to bless her within the revelation that in God's Kingdom there is an *abundance of life* and all she needed was to sow in faith from the little that she had.

The Bible encourages us to make seed sowing a habit in order for us to always be in a position of harvesting. The way I see it is that God's creation serves us as an example of how the heavenly Kingdom is like. You see in the natural, different plants grow in different seasons. Each season has its own kind of plants that grow. Put another way, there are plants that only thrive in a particular season. Now in advising us to be habitual sowers, the teaching is set to put us in a position of harvesting in not just one kind of season only.

The parallel of this is that we are not just to be sowers of money and then have an abundance of wealth but lack in other things that God has for us. No-o-o...! We are to constantly be sowing-in a variety of seeds, e.g. sow money *today*, sow food *tomorrow*, sow peace, health, kindness and love *everyday*, and sow the seeds of the fruits of the spirit as often as His grace guides us.

Lesson #3: God's Grace

We can hardly separate the concept of *seeds-sowing* from *God's-grace*. God had placed the woman of Zarephath in that particular place in-order for her to take care of Elijah. It is not necessarily that she was there because of her obedience but by grace; God hand-picked her to be the one to experience His divine provision. To start with, she was a gentile. As such, she was clearly not a person who believed in God. But when grace came her way she noticed Him and received her 'Salvation'.

[93]Jesus later on talked about this woman, thereby affirming further that what happened to her was an act of grace. This woman lived in a town far from Israel, a place where they were foreign to God, where they worshiped foreign gods, a place that was ruled by Jezebel's father who was a high priest of Baal worshipers. It is by grace that God hand-picked this woman to whom death had become a frequent visitor in her life. She had already experienced the loss of her husband and because of the draught, death must had become a norm to her as she witnessed all vegetation and livestock die around her. Add to this her real-time experience of slowly seeing her life-sustaining food storage diminishing to an end. She was fully awake to the fact that, just as death had taken everything from her, it was finally coming for her and her son.

It is eminent therefore that grace covered this woman and ordered her steps to be just where she was when Elijah arrived in the town in order for them to meet. It was not sheer coincidence...! She was not there because she was obeying God's voice; as a gentile, she did not even know God's voice. God literary set her up...! He set her up for a lesson of tithing and seed sowing in God's Kingdom.

[93] Luke 4:26

We know that this woman was a sinner and did not get blessed on her own merit because when later on her son died, she thought she was being *punished* by the God whom she had then gotten to know. She did not realise that she was again being set up to know God. We see again here that when death knocked at her door, the opportunity was for her to see God, not death. Elijah prayed for her son, and he was raised from death. That was when this woman's eyes were truly opened up to the awareness that the Almighty Living God is the most high God, the provider and giver of life.

Her own gods had never helped her during *famine*. Because these other gods always want a religious sacrifice of some sort when coming to them for help, I can only imagine how she must had sacrificed the little she had, praying to them for providence and to keep her livestock from dying. We are not told of how and when her husband died, but I can imagine that she must had prayed to her gods to keep him alive in the least, if not raise him back to life and not let her fall into being a widow.

Mind you it must had been a very hard situation to be a widow back in those days especially when one had no male adult child to represent her in legal and social circles as women had no say in most things, by law. Fortunately for her, just like every one of us in numerous instances, she experienced God's grace that chose her without her even knowing about it. This grace gave her food to sustain her life and that of her son, and also literary gave life back to her son.

Hard economic times should not depress us once we are under God's covenant of grace, the covenant where our hope is in the Lord, where we have entered His rest, where we get whatsoever blessings we get based on Jesus' finished works on the cross rather than on the basis of what we do. The global *famine* has put us all in the same situation as the lady of Zarephath, together with our personal moments or instances whereby we go through some sort of shortage of supply.

We need to learn from her, that we need not worry (as Jesus affirmed), about food, cloth or shelter, and other things of this world because God already knows about our needs and desires, just as He knew for this woman. Rather, we are to [94]seek the Kingdom of God first as the Bible says. When Elijah asked her to make for him FIRST the bread, which required of her an exercise of faith, her obedience was an express form of seeking God's Kingdom FIRST. And Jesus says that the [94]rest of *these things* will follow. What things? Well, the food, clothes,

[94] Matthew 6:33

shelter, money, love, and all other things that we worry about...The abundant lifestyle...!

We are to seek God's Kingdom then as our first priority. We are to trust His *Word* that the rest of things will follow. In so doing, we are not to worry about how things look like in the natural. We are not to be wary of the natural state of being because we have already stepped out of the natural by virtue of being under His grace. We are already operating under the supernatural realm, because there is nothing natural about God's grace my dear. God's grace is supernatural...!

Come to think of it...What is *famine* ANYWAY to a grace-covered believer? - [95]Isaac, the grace-given son of Abraham, sowed seeds during *famine* and reaped a 100 fold...! That is probably more than you normally reap even when there is no *famine*.

As a thought of caution, we cannot afford to mistake the preceding seed-sowing concept with a misconception that we are creating our own abundance. The over-riding authority is grace. Jesus came to give us an abundant life. Without Him we cannot experience that abundant life. All there is to it is God honouring us to operate under His original blessing for mankind, the blessing of "...replenish the earth and subdue

[95] Genesis 26:12

it…" God's grace is about taking us back to His original plan and out of the covenant of the law; back to relying on God and operating under His blessings.

Lesson #4: Submission is for our own good

God is the creator of the universe. He owns it all. He has it all, much more that we can imagine. So when God asks for something from us, it is not because he is in need of that which He asks for. Rather, He is simply setting us up to receive from Him. In guiding us to sow a *seed* of whatsoever we have in order for it to multiply, He is reiterating His love for us and intention to bless it saying [96]"…be fruitful and multiply…"

Why does He not just create the things from scratch and give us without asking from us? That He can, but I think He meant for us to enter into His rest and see that He really did finish creation and set everything to reproduce and that he blessed us to be part of "…replenish the earth…" Having already created us in His own likeness, He meant for us to share in, be part of, enjoy, and continue His master-piece work of creation. What he was saying was simply a reminder to us to not eat both the *fruits* and *seeds* after harvesting, but to please replant the seeds so that life may self-sustainably continue. By asking from us, He is simply setting us up to receive His blessings. The receiving

[96]   Genesis 1:22, 28

part requires of us to be submissive and exercise our faith in Him.

On a light note it was like saying, "I do not have to create over and over again whenever you have eaten every *fruit* because I have done and completed a perfect job. That is why I have entered into my resting day. All that is left for you *gods,* and for which I have empowered and blessed you to, is replenish, exercise dominion, and co-operate with the creation."

Looking closely into the account of the woman of Zarephath, Elijah symbolises Jesus (in a veiled form) asking for bread from this woman, yet we already know he is the bread of life. What is He doing then, asking the woman to give Him what he already has an abundance of? He is simply setting her up, making her sow her seed in a super-fertile ground where the bread will be given to her in more than enough supply.

Besides her submission bringing more life to her family by way of having sufficient continued supply of food, the very encounter may be seen at a spiritual level as being synonymous to her moment of receiving Salvation, i.e. eternal life. This eternal life is the complete opposite of the death she anticipated before meeting Elijah. She did not earn it; - she just had to be willing to receive it, and so is the case with every one of us. Take note how Jesus in the unveiled form (Elijah) repeats in different words the same original blessing of "...be fruitful and multiply..." with [97]reference to the flour and oil that the woman had used.

In another yet similar context, we can recall the story of the [98]Samaritan woman. She too was a sinner, undeserving of God's grace. Jesus asked for water from her, yet He is the living water. Once again here, He was just setting her up for a blessing.

[99]When the 5000 people were to be fed, the same miraculously phenomenal blessing of "...be fruitful and multiply..." happened, i.e. Jesus asked for the food that was available (2 fish and 5 loaves of bread), blessed it, and it multiplied to become more than enough for everyone. [100]This similarly happened with the 4000 people as well.

Remember too when Job was experiencing a great *famine* in his life and it seemed like he had no *seed* to sow. By grace he was guided to *sow a seed* that he was all along not seeing. [101]God told Job to *pray for his friends* and only after that did he get to be blessed again. More than before, the way I see it is that

[97]   I Kings 17:14
[98]   John 4:1-26
[99]   Matthew 14: 13-21
[100] Matthew 15:29-39
[101] Job 42:10

there before, Job was a man whose righteousness was based on the law as he often made sacrifices for his children. Yes he hated evil and loved good but as mentioned earlier on, he was apparently not aware of the full measure of God's grace in his life.

In all the afore-going accounts, *submission* is the key ingredient to the activation of *God's blessing* of multiplication and fruitfulness. The two facets operate under the umbrella of God's universally available grace. It is upon us to exercise our freedom of choice to the effect of receiving God's blessings by being submissive to Him and His ordained authorities. This choice is squarely pivoted on our faith and trust in the Almighty Living God, from whom all good things come. After all, it all pans out to be for our own good and for the good of our loved ones.

(6): Mary

[Luke 1: 26-38]

An Angel Tells about the Birth of Jesus

²⁶One month later God sent the angel Gabriel to the town of Nazareth in Galilee ²⁷with a message for a virgin named Mary. She was engaged to Joseph from the family of King David. ²⁸The angel greeted Mary and said, "You are truly blessed! The Lord is with you."

²⁹Mary was confused by the angel's words and wondered what they meant. ³⁰Then the angel told Mary, "Don't be afraid! God is pleased with you, ³¹and you will have a son. His name will be Jesus. ³²He will be great and will be called the Son of God Most High. The Lord God will make him king, as his ancestor David was. ³³He will rule the people of Israel forever, and his kingdom will never end."

³⁴Mary asked the angel, "How can this happen? I am not married!"

³⁵The angel answered, "The Holy Spirit will come down to you, and God's power will come over you. So your child will be called the holy Son of God. ³⁶Your relative Elizabeth is also going to have a son, even though she is old. No one thought she could ever have a baby, but in three months she will have a son. ³⁷Nothing is impossible for God!"

³⁸Mary said, "I am the Lord's servant! Let it happen as you have said." And the angel left her.

Luke 1:26 - 38 [CEV]

Hail Mary !

Hail Mary, full of grace,
the Lord is with you.
Blessed are you among women,
and blessed is the fruit
of your womb JESUS.
Holy Mary, Mother of God...!
[Luke 1: 28-35; 42-48]

Believe

*A*ccording to *Encarta English dictionary* and *Thesaurus*, 'believe' means to trust, have faith in, be certain of, have confidence in, accept as true, and rely on.

Oh how there is a remedy for all sins but none for disbelieve...!

LESSONS from Mary's life

Lesson #1: Having faith in God

What a beautiful story of obedience...! Mary totally *submitted* to God, even when it seemed like it would jeopardize her love life and mess up her good reputation; she was a virgin engaged to Joseph. Imagine how she was to explain her being pregnant and still claim her story of being a virgin to be true. Surely in the natural, it would have been impossible for Mary to tell her story and have Joseph convinced it was true.

At face-value, the angel's message sounds so unbelievable. From a mortal's level of understanding, it also sounds like it would come with some unpleasant consequences if it were to be true. Yet Mary believed!

Thank you Mary for your exemplary faith!

What if you put yourself in Mary's shoes?

Would you have believed the angel? Remember some of the women in *Part I* who failed to believe. They too were presented with God's *Word*, but they could not believe it. Just to refresh your memory on a few of them:

- Eve did not believe that the fruit would really kill them but it did.

- Lot's wife did not believe that they really should not look back; - Even though she was told not to, she must have thought to herself "what harm will it do ... to just look?" Kill you ... That is exactly what happened to her !

- The worst was Jezebel, who was so blinded by disbelief that it made her stubborn till she died, having had so many opportunities to repent.

Yet Mary believed a message that had never been heard of, a message that was and still is scientifically impossible; a virgin falling pregnant without involvement of a mortal being. Seriously who would believe that? Well, Mary did...! She had so much faith in God and she knew that whatsoever God says is true as He is incapable of lying. She knew that if God gives you a promise, it will come to pass even if it looks impossible; simply because it is from God then it means it will happen, some-how, some-way, some-day...!

Just believe and God will sort out the rest...

God sorted out everything for her to the effect that she did not have to do anything else. Of utmost importance, God sorted out Joseph for her when he was planning to divorce her as a consequence of the divine pregnancy.

Similarly, all that is requested of us is to believe God's *Word*. Just that! The 'HOW?'s, 'WHERE?'s, and 'WHEN?'s are for God; they are not for us to figure out. And Mary definitely got that part right; she did her part of believing God's *Word* and left the rest up to Him.

God's part is basically the rest of the things that come after believing His *Word*. As for Mary, these things included, among others:

(1) [102]Confirming to Joseph that her conception was supernatural; that Mary was still a virgin. This was accomplished by sending an angel to Joseph.

(2) He made sure that Jesus was safe from harm, including [103]Herod who sought to kill Him. This was also accomplished by sending an angel.

(3) Taught Jesus on how to be a [104]Priest at an early age of 12 years.

(4) He saw to it that [105]Jesus succeeded in fulfilling His calling to deliver mankind by going to the cross submissively.

Mary could not have been able to accomplish any of these things; they were for the almighty God to do. You can imagine just how frustrated she would have ended up being in trying to do God's work. She would definitely have robbed herself off the peace and joy of having been specially chosen and uniquely blessed by God.

By obeying God you get to be blessed and to be a blessing to others.

---

[102] Matthew 1: 18-25
[103] Matthew 2: 13-16
[104] Luke 2: 39-51
[105] Luke 22: 42; Hebrews 5: 7-8

Very simply put, our role is to just believe God's *Word*. This applies to all situations. Whatsoever God calls you to or intends to use you for, your part is simply to believe and surrender the rest to Him. One such common and general call for most women is to be mothers to children. These children are the future of human race. Our part as women is to simply believe God's *Word* concerning our children. [106]God says that it is not up to us to write their life story...Our part is to just believe...!

Lesson #2: Readiness to *submit*

If God wants to use you, just say yes. Do not look at your situation and say no simply because it looks impossible to you. Your 'yes' will give birth to unbelievable blessings, not just for you but for other people as well. Remember also the many times that Jesus said, [107]"... especially when it seems like the *Word* is leading you into trouble ... when persecutions come because of the *Word*."

Lesson #3: It's not about *Law* but *Grace*

When God calls you, it's never about you, but always about His Word

---

[106] Luke 8: 50; Matthew 21: 15-16; Psalms 8: 2; Matthew 18: 10
[107] Mark 4: 16-17; Matthew 13: 21; John 15: 18-21

God called Mary to the wonderful opportunity of being the woman with the most blessed womb, to be the only woman whose body carried its creator, the only woman who became a mother to her creator, who nursed her creator. The poignant question is, what is it that Mary did for her to qualify her for such a blessing? Unbelievable as it is, Mary did nothing special or extraordinary for her to qualify for the blessing. Nevertheless, she simply believed God's *Word* when her call came.

The angel came to tell her a *Word* from God and all that Mary did was believe. It took so much wisdom from her to believe such a message and from what we already know, wisdom comes from God. In *I Corinthians I*, wisdom is translated not to just being a *thing* but also to the *affirmation* that wisdom is God.

> *"But of Him are ye in Christ Jesus, who of God is made unto us wisdom, and righteousness, and sanctification, and redemption:"* - I Corinthians I: 30 [KJV].

Therefore it took God in her to be able to choose to believe the *Word* that the angel delivered to her. It is by grace that we believe; it is not by our natural understanding that we believe but rather by God's empowerment on us. That wisdom in her made it possible for her to recognize the underlying fact that the naturally impossible *Word* that she had just received had nothing to do with her (her ability or level of faith), but that she was just being used by God as His servant for a good course.

God is Wisdom, Jesus is Wisdom, and the Holy Spirit is Wisdom

---

If it was about her, then she would have been required to have a certain amount of faith to be able to believe God's *Word*. She would have had to figure out how to make that *Word* come to pass, most probably spend endless sleepless nights trying to figure it all out. Besides figuring out how it would be possible for her to conceive while she was still a virgin, she would also probably have been required to be able to make Jesus believe that he was the son of God and guide Him on how to save mankind. Wow! What a burden that would have been! Just imagining about all the things that would have been required of her makes me feel sorry for her already.

If that was to be the case, then God would have subjected Mary under the law, which is a system meant to show human weakness. Needless to say, all that would then have happened was that Mary would have seen just how weak she was as a human being because she would never have figured out a way of making the *Word* of God come to pass. In her mortal capacity, she would also never have been able to lead Jesus to the cross. No sober mother is equipped to do that.

But wisdom showed Mary that it was all about God, and that her part was only to believe and leave the rest up to Him. And since [108]God is no respecter of man, whatsoever He did in Mary's case, He can accomplish in our individual cases as well only if we quit trying to do His job and also realize that it is not about us.

This book is my testimony of that experience that Mary had. I too heard a *Word* from God in me saying, "from now on you will minister God's *Word* through writing". And now that you are reading this very book at this very moment, that should be sure evidence that I chose to believe.

In my particular case, that massage sounded impossible because I was looking at me. When I focused on me, this is what I saw: Firstly, I cannot be a writer because I have a terrible problem when it comes to spelling even the most of simple words. I just cannot seem to remember the right spelling of words, which is why I often prefer calling people instead of sending text messages or responding to emails. This is because it is very frustrating for me to look up the spelling of almost every word

[108] Acts 10:34

that I write. In the natural, that disqualifies me from attempting to preach God's *Word* through written media.

At the initial stage, even some very close people who have always been supportive and reassuring tried to talk me out of the call; it has never been done in the family, it will be a waste of time, your spelling is horrible, how will you do this and how will you do that...? Against all the odds, I chose to listen not to the natural but to just believe the *Word*; knowing very well that it is not about me but rather about Him who called me ... it is not about what I can or cannot do, but rather what he wants done through me ... it is not about what I have, but rather whom I have in me ... All I had to do was to accept the call and believe.

On that note, just in case you come across some spelling mistakes in this and my yet to be published future books or literature works, simply attribute them mistakes to the respective editor(s); Rest assured that if they were mine, they would definitely have been worse and bordering catastrophe...!

Secondly I thought to myself that since the *Word* for me was to write books that would teach about, and explain God's *Word*, where will I start? Letting alone the fact that I did not even have any topic in mind, what was worse at the time was that I did not even know about the *Word* of God to a point that I would qualify to teach it to others. I still needed teaching myself.

Because I looked so much to me, I then decided to do it my way, in the only way that it looked possible. So I began to write a book about beauty, with numerous topics and advise on each one of them. I picked beauty because in my mind, that was what I considered myself to be most qualified in, i.e. in the natural. I have amassed so much knowledge and experience in the hair, skin, nails, and in relaxation therapy. So that seemed like the only field that made sense to me. Then that voice which spiritually guides us was just disagreeing with me, until I finally surrendered to it. Once I did that, ideas started flowing faster than I could type them down, especially considering that at that time I was critically slow in typing.

The moment I surrendered, God revealed to me that the call was not about me, but about Him. He just wants to teach His *Word* through me. As I set out to do it, the whole ball of wax became increasingly more and more clear that it was not me who was set to do the teaching; my role immediately ended at the very moment when I believed and accepted to be His servant.

My story is not so special because you too and everyone else has had a similar experience. God is always calling out for His children. In whatsoever it is that God has called you to do, always remember that He does not expect any help from you in order to accomplish the mission. All He wants is for you to believe and *submit* to Him!

What happens if one chooses not to believe?

Whether you choose to believe or not, the fact remains that it's not about you but Him. In case you choose not to believe, God will simply call out another person with the same *Word*. So if Mary for instance had chosen not to believe, that would not have been a problem for God because He would just go ahead and send the same *Word* to a different woman and His purpose would still have been fulfilled. The only one who misses out is the one who refuses to believe, not God.

Let us look at afew stories that feature all or most of the angles just discussed, that is, God sending a *Word* that is impossible in the natural ... that it is not about you ... and what happens if we try assisting Him:

Story #1: Abraham

Just like Mary, Abraham's news made no sense in the natural; the news that he would become a father of many nations at a time when he had not even been able to have just one child with his wife Sarah. Good enough, Abraham believed God, and indeed he became the father of so many nations. The Bible says that the moment we are born again, we (spiritually) become sons and daughters of Abraham. Add to this the fact that even in the natural, Abraham's descendants through Isaac are countless.

It is not about the person called but about God

By the way, it was not about Abraham as God had earlier on called his father, [109]Terah, to use him to fulfill the same *Word*. However, Abraham's father decided to settle down half-way along the journey to Canaan. That is why God then chose Abraham later on. If his father had believed till the *Word* was fulfilled, then today we would imperatively be called the sons and daughters of Terah.

Trying to assist God in fulfilling His Word

What makes Mary's account so great is that she never tried to help God in anyway. If she did, I imagine she would have sought to timeously seduce Joseph to have sex with her right from the day she had the news so that she would conceive as that was the only known natural way. As we can all guess, that child she

[109] Genesis 11: 31-32

would have conceived from such a stunt would not have been Jesus.

In contrast to Mary, and due to a great influence from his wife, Abraham tried to assist God in fulfilling His *Word* by sleeping with Hagar (Sarah's slave). And sure enough just as it would have been if Mary had conceived from Joseph, in which case it would NOT have been the promised messiah, so it was with Abraham. The child that they got was definitely NOT the one God had promised. He was a totally different outcome because of trying to help God.

Similarly, so many of us have the tendency of trying to help God whenever He presents His *Word* to us. Then we wonder why the results we get do not even closely match with His *Word*.

Story #2: Others

Remember [110]Moses who was called to lead the Israelites in God's mission to deliver them from slavery in Egypt, yet he was a stammerer? Remember [111]David, a young herd's boy without military training or armour going ahead to defeat Goliath? Most of all, remember [112]Jesus, the "carpenter's son" being the

---

[110]   Genesis 3:10; Genesis 4:10
[111]   I Samuel 17: 41-51
[112]   Mark 6:3

messiah, saving the entire world?

Naturally it is just not possible to believe God's *Word*, but His grace is there to help us believe. What is essential is that, once we believe, we should leave it all up to Him until His *Word* is fulfilled, rather than getting distracted and settling for what IS NOT His *Word* along the way.

Do not get tempted to assist Him...!

If you have been diagnosed with any incurable disease, God sends news to you saying, [113]'by His strips you were healed...'.

If you are grieving the loss of a loved one and have lost your peace of mind as a result, He promises you [114]'peace that surpasses all understanding...'.

If you have sinned, however big your sin seems to you and are tormented by guilt, God says, [115]'I do not condemn you...'.

If you are a Christian but no matter how hard you try, every now and again you *miss the mark* and you feel like God is disappointed with you, the *Word* says, [116]'God sees you as righteous as Jesus Christ is...'.

If you are looking forward to death so that you can go to

---

[113] Isaiah 53: 5
[114] Philippians 4: 7
[115] Romans 8: 1; Psalms 34: 22
[116] Ephesians 1: 6; 1 Corinthians 1: 30; 2 Corinthians 5: 21; Romans 5: 17; Philippians 3: 8-9

heaven and finally be like Jesus; be as whole as He is, the Word says, [117]'as He is, so are you in this world.'

Yes - it makes no sense naturally but it is not about you. There are so many people that God sends that same *Word* to and those who open up to His grace are made able to believe such news and benefit a lot from them. In the process, God receives honor and glory because everyone gets to see that His *Word* is true, alive, reliable, and that God really is who He says He *is*.

Lesson #4: Do not be afraid...!

Where fear is, there will be submission...!

The above statement is like a universal law that cannot be changed, whether we chose to believe it or not. The general advice from God to us is that we need to *fear* (<u>revere</u>) Him. I believe that is because we normally (by *default settings...*) *submit* to whatsoever or whosoever we look up to. So if God is the only one we *fear*, then He will be the only one we *submit* to. It is through our submission to God that we will be empowered to follow His ways, which are centered on the expectation for us to *submit* to all the God-ordained authorities in our lives and to do so in a Godly way.

You can imagine what Mary's possible range of fears would

[117]　I John 4: 17

have been, for example, the fear that what the angel was saying would not come to be, the fear that Joseph would leave her, the fear of what the parents, relatives, friends and the community in general would think of her, and so on. Mary must have *feared* the Lord besides everything else. Because of that, she gained divine wisdom that in turn guided her into handling the situation she was in the way she did. As it is proven in Mary's story, the Bible says:

> 'The steps of a good man are ordered by the LORD, and He delights in his way' - Psalms 37: 23 [NKJV]

When Mary gained wisdom as a result of fearing only the Lord, in actual fact what happened is that she had God in her (God is wisdom). When God comes in us, He comes-in in the form of Spirit, which means that Mary then gained the Spirit of the LORD in her. In the physical, this Spirit 'ordered her steps'.

Whatsoever is in you has the power to control you; both internally and externally!

This is also true for your body organs; they have the power to control you. For instance if your lungs decide to stop functioning today, it does not matter how much you were determined to go out and do whatever you had planned to do; their status of not functioning properly will immediately reorder your steps to a route that is different from the one you had planned. Suddenly you will have to go to hospital, for example, something that was not in your *To-Do* List.

Similarly in return for only fearing God, His Spirit gets inside us and controls us. We become possessed by the Spirit of the Lord and that is how he orders our steps. We start doing things that we otherwise would not have done if we were relying on our own evaluation or judgment of things. We start knowing things that we naturally would not be able to know, and that is what happened (and still happens) to God's prophets. They spoke of things that they naturally would not know of, definitely not from their intelligence. They spoke of things that would happen in the future and those things eventually happened. As of now, some more things are yet still destined to happen exactly as prophesied.

Is it that the prophets were very intelligent people, people who could see into the future? Absolutely not...! Their distinguished and consistent impact was only attributable to the fact that all the prophecies were not from them *per se* but from the LORD; it was the LORD speaking through them and the LORD our God knows everything - He knows everything that has been lined up to happen right from the beginning, through present, all the way to eternity. He even knows all the people who will go to heaven and he knows those who will not; nothing can surprise God.

If we fear only God, the same thing happens to us. We start functioning in a *supernatural* way, not because we have supernatural abilities but because we become *possessed* by the one who has supernatural abilities.

[118] *Supernatural* means:

Unearthly, psychic, unnatural, magic, eerie, mystical, paranormal, clairvoyant, miraculous, telepathic, intuitive, second-sighted...

[119] *Possess* means:

Influence, dominate, occupy, have power over, hold, seize, take over, control, own, retain, enjoy...

Therefore whatsoever you fear will possess you.

Substituting the word *possess* with its synonyms we obtain statements like:

Whatsoever you fear will *influence* you.

Whatsoever you fear will *dominate* you.

Whatsoever you fear will *occupy* you.

Whatsoever you fear will *have power over* you.

[118]   Thesaurus: English (U.K)
[119]   Thesaurus: English (U.K)

> Whatsoever you fear will *hold* you.
>
> (...remember the [120]*strong holds*...?)

...and the list continues...!

Impact of being possessed

Have you ever done something and later on said, 'I really do not know what got into me in order for me to do that'? We usually figuratively say that the *wrong-*, and at times the *right-* buttons on us were pressed as if we are robots. We may say, 'so and so just knows how to push the wrong buttons in me'. That is usually the case after we find ourselves behaving in a way that is outside of our character or norm.

Well, we are not robots and so there really are no 'buttons' to push on us. The truth is that there are things that happen in our lives that have the power to trigger the release of what is already in us. If the spirit of God is in you, evil things that happen around you will trigger the release of the spirit, which will then control you in making you do what it wants. For instance, you may come across a person who is experiencing *lack*, be it the lack of money or whatsoever else that may be short supply in that person's life. That very situation has the power to unleash the spirit within that person. The spirit will

---

[120] 2 Corinthians 10:3-5; Numbers 13:17-19

then take control of that person, leading him/her to do something towards taking away the *lack* and giving abundance.

Remember: *Lack is a form of evil - it started after the fall of man* [121]*(Adam and Eve) when they became naked ... lack of 'clothes'.*

At times the possessing situation is not so obvious, for example, where a person may be looking like he/she has everything yet they are struggling in life. Naturally you would not know about what the person is going through but the spirit of God who knows everything will lead you to helping such a person.

On the contrary if we do not *fear* God, we automatically fear the evil one, and so his evil spirit(s) possess us and make us do evil things. Basically they make us do the opposite of what God says we must do. Many of the people in jail for gruesome murders can attest to, 'I really don't know what took over me during that moment when I killed that person'. For some, it goes as far as not even having a memory of the incident. The latter cases are actually extreme situations where the evil spirit takes total control of the mind and body. The main reason why they end up doing what they do is because of the fear they have for the devil, who in exchange for their fear possesses them.

[121] Genesis 2:25

King David, a man who feared the LORD our God and was possessed by Him once said:

"*¹The LORD is my shepherd; I shall not want. ²He maketh me to lie down in green pastures: he leadeth me beside the still waters. ³He restoreth my soul: he leadeth me in the paths of righteousness for His name's sake.⁴Yea, though I walk through the valley of the shadow of death, I will fear no evil: for thou art with me; thy rod and thy staff they comfort me. ⁵Thou preparest a table before me in the presence of mine enemies: thou anointest my head with oil; my cup runneth over. ⁶Surely goodness and mercy shall follow me all the days of my life: and I will dwell in the house of the LORD for ever.*"

Psalms 23 [KJV]

When reading this prayer I realized just how possessed king David was. Even the prayer that he was praying was not from his natural understanding; it was God speaking through him. He was praying in the spirit. The way the prayer is ordered is very amazing.

Firstly he proclaims the LORD as his shepherd, affirming that he 'shall not want'. This indicates the totality of divine provision in which there is no lack whatsoever.

In the second verse he praises the nature of the divine provision, as in, it not just pastures, but *green pastures* and beside *still* (Peaceful...!) *waters*. This reflects the abundance and proximity of the divine provision that he receives without straining ... in lay terms, he as the Shepherd's sheep does not have to walk long distances (i.e. struggle or toil) in order to drink water after getting fully fed.

In the third verse, he caps the safety of his soul under His care and affirms his awareness of the fact that the LORD orders his steps in righteousness, not for his sake but rather for His name's sake. David knew it was all not about him but ultimately about the LORD.

Then David gives us an even more intriguing revelation when he goes on to proclaim the supremacy of LORD's presence above everything else in his life; "Yea though I walk through the valley of the shadow of death" ... the wisdom in him made it possible for him to recognize that evil had no power to kill but only to scare. That is why he categorically refers to the *valley of the shadow of death*, and not the *valley of death*. A shadow in itself is like a scare-crow or a toothless dog, i.e. unlike the object casting it, the shadow in itself poses no harm. It is like an illusion. A shadow of death for us could be anything that is from the devil; anything that is life threatening since he is opposed to life. A good example is an instance where one is diagnosed with an 'incurable' disease ... That disease is not death or a death sentence in itself, but rather a mere evil shadow of death.

As a follow-up, David says, "I will *fear* no evil" ... meaning 'I will not fear what is coming from the devil', 'I will not fear the doctor's adverse diagnosis' ... because if I choose to *fear* it, I will be giving it power over me, allowing it to control me, to hold me captive, to occupy me, and to order my steps ...!

Then he states his reason for not fearing any evil; "for you are with me Lord" ... he is saying 'because you have possessed me', 'you have taken control of me'; 'your presence in me Lord' is the reason why I fear no evil.

Lastly, David then continues to show how his choice of not fearing evil has impacted on his life. He talks about the effects of being possessed ... being 'controlled', saying, "Thy rod and thy staff comfort me" ... he is simply saying that God has total control over him by: (1) controlling him with the staff that shepherds use to pull sheep when they tend to take a different direction from the rest of the flock, and on top of that, (2) with the aid of a rod, the LORD controls what happens to him externally - He controls what can and cannot come into contact with him; any evil. In the context of sheep, the evil includes foxes and wolves that want to kill the sheep. For us it is anything that threatens to kill us, physically or spiritually - Our Lord is in full control of that as He drives it away from us.

Moreover in this prayer, I see how much possessed David was because he refers to the Lord as his Shepherd. Notice that only one who knows the future could do that because, years later, the very God he was referring to as a shepherd came down to earth in human form (Jesus) and referred to Himself as a shepherd, declaring:

"I am the good shepherd...." - John 10: 11 [NKJV]

Similarly then, it is very clear that Mary was possessed by God's spirit because she feared God. It was not from her ability but rather the ability of the one who possessed her that she believed the massage that was naturally unbelievable. Therefore our correct submissiveness too starts with the *fear* of God.

So why does God reserve fear only for Himself?

That is because when we fear God we give Him a place of honour as the mighty LORD that He *is*. On the contrary, when we fear some*thing* or someone else we give that place of honour to it / him / her and that makes God very jealous. [122]We serve a jealous God, jealous about us because He loves us so dearly. Fearing God is therefore hereby interpreted to mean *revering* and *honouring* Him as opposed to being *afraid* of Him.

The place of honour refers to our worshiping God. This means that when we fear other things, we worship them as we then put them on God's sit, thereby saying that they are greater than God. We implicitly make that thing / her / him our god. This is what the Bible says about that:

> "For thou shalt worship no other god: for the LORD, whose name is Jealous, is a jealous God." - Exodus 34: 14 [KJV].

The bottom line here is that fear is a form of worship and the only one worthy of that is God. As the very first

[122] Zechariah 1:14

commandment is 'worship no god but me', I believe that the 10 commandments are in the order of importance and that is why worship constitutes the *Number 1* commandment.

What not to fear

The sum total of what not to fear is simply anything or anyone that is not God.

Our most common fear

We differ in the things we fear as people because of many different reasons. Nevertheless, a general fear that is common worldwide is the fear associated with money, be it the fear of lacking in money, or the fear of losing it once we have it. The diverse results of that fear are proportionally evident throughout the world. To mention but a few examples, we fear not having enough money to sustain our lives; atleast money for food, shelter and clothing. So for most of us, the fear of money insufficiency has been passed on to us from our parents since the time when we were young. It has therefore seemingly taken roots because this has been happening throughout many generations.

As discussed above, we see that because of the fear of monetary inadequacy, we have given money the power to control us in the choices we make. Take for instance the choice of careers (does the job pay well financially?), the car you drive (how much money do you have?), the location and type of house you live in, the places or stores you shop in, which hospital to go to whenever you are feeling sick, which restaurants to dine in ... and unfortunately even the choice of who to marry is at times pegged onto envisaged cash-flow extrapolations or anticipations.

This tendency has corrupted even the upbringing process of our children over the years. Parents are very proud of their children if they become doctors, lawyers, engineers, and so on ... Why? - Because the perception is that there is more money in this or that career. So their being proud of their children is a *(fear) feeling* induced by *(lack of)* money. There is no greater level of slavery than that, and blessed are the parents who encourage their children to make career decisions based on what they *love* doing.

The *Word* of God warns us against giving money power over us ...making it our master...! [123]You cannot be the slave of both God and money.

This reiterates what we discussed earlier, that you implicitly

---

[123] Matthew 6: 24; Luke 16: 13

worship whatsoever you fear. Take note that [124]worship is broadly synonymous to terms such as *reverence*, *adore*, *devotion*, and *love*. Therefore by *worshipping* whatsoever you *fear*, you practically place it in God's position; revering, adoring, being devoted to, and being in love with it in lieu of God. As the fear of God is the starting point of being possessed by Him, so is the fear of money the starting point of being possessed by evil. In other words, the *Love* of God is the beginning of wisdom ... and the *fear* of money is the root of evil.

Dear Mary,

Greetings to you blessed and holy mother of God...!

I can only vaguely imagine how you felt like when you got the never-heard-of news of your conception. Thank you for submitting to God's Word.

Yours in adoration,

Pypie.

---

[124] Thesaurus: English (U.K).

Part 3

The Devil's attack on women

Introduction

*C*ome to think of it; what if God created human beings to be like a house? In that context the man would be a complete house with a strong foundation and roof, and a woman would only be the pillars (or reinforcement walls). In that context the role of the woman may look insignificant at face value until one awakens to the fact that a house, strong and well-built as it may be, stands no chance of stable existence on its own. Supportive as the pillars may be, they too are of no use if they are not supporting the house. The house and pillars are symbiotic rather than mutually exclusive to each other, and so are a husband and wife.

The devil seems to have figured that out long time ago. By virtue of being aware of women's influential power over men, he does not necessarily have to target men with his deceptive ways and means. By targeting the pillars (women), he effectively lays his ambushes on the houses (men). Hopefully by dedicating this section of the book to throwing some light onto a sample of the devil's attacks (ploys), we may be better prepared in discerning them and striving towards rendering his mission impossible.

It looks like women, according to the devil's silent testimony, have always been the *weakest link*. This may be true from one perspective, especially when we revisit the Biblical accounts of some women such as [125]Eve and [126]Mrs. Job. In both cases, the devil succeeded in getting the women to act under his influence. At the next phase, both women tried to influence their respective Husbands. The decisions made and actions taken by the husbands eventually determined the devil's success and failure in his intentions, respectively. As discussed in preceding sections, this affirms the *supremacy* of husbands over their wives within the marriage covenant. However, *supremacy* does not necessarily have to be interpreted to mean *strength*.

From another perspective, it can be argued that the devil tends to attack women first because they are the *strongest link*. By conquering the woman, the devil knows he has an edge towards conquering the man as well because of the formidable *power of influence* that women generally have over men. In very many instances, the devil has succeeded in using that strategy. In that sense we can say that, even the devil himself acknowledges and appreciates women's power. To *bring-down* a strong house, the easiest route is to first *bring-down* the pillars

[125] Genesis 2: 21 – 23; Genesis 3
[126] JOB 1 and JOB 2: 1-10

and/or any other support structure. In that sense therefore, women are stronger than men.

It is with the afore-going knowledge and understanding that the devil has constantly attacked women. He is still very busy at it even today and it does not seem like he is set to stop any time soon. We are in a battle field. The devil is continually laying his ambush on us in the hope of *bringing*-mankind-*down* using all sorts of strategies. This section is dedicated to highlighting some of the devil's strategies so that, as women, we can be well prepared, alert, and sufficiently armed as we take him on.

<u>CAUTION</u>: It is NOT by our *strength*, but rather by our *faith* and *trust* in God's grace that we CAN win this battle...!

Attack 1:

To prevent or stagnate proliferation of life

God's first blessing for mankind to 'multiply'...!

As women, we have been entrusted by God to carry and nurse our children. He placed the seed in the men and then He made us the ground where the seed can grow. We are to take this task as serious as it really is, not letting the devil rob us off God's first and main blessing to mankind; multiplication. As it was in the garden whereby the devil deceived the woman, he still is doing the same today. Women all over the world have been deceived over and over again by the devil. Most of us still cannot see that one of his primary goals is to stop the first blessing; he wants the opposite of all that God blessed us with.

For every of God's blessings and intents for mankind, there seems to be an exact parallel and opposite of the devils mission. For instance, [127]God says ... be fruitful, and multiply, and replenish the earth, and subdue it ... Then the devil on the contrary works towards making sure that instead of multiplying and being fruitful, we abort children, kill each other in wars, spread killer diseases, stress (lower chances of conception), have unhealthy eating habits (that may even lead to infertility), bear no fruits, and so on. Instead of replenishing the earth, we end up neglecting the planet, destroying forests (fires and cutting of trees without replacements ... and then eventually complain of global warming), destroying the marine life ... cumulatively choking the life of the planet.

It is our responsibility to be on guard. We need beware that the devil is trying to use women in order to keep us all from enjoying the blessings that God gave us.

---

[127] Genesis 1:28

Red Flag #1:
Media lies about women's beauty

In order to stop us from multiplying, the devil has inspired people to come up with all sorts of ploys that prevent or lower the chances of conception. The media has been his main platform from where he gets so many women deceived especially because they cannot seem to see that he is behind it all. The media has for instance spread the idea that unless a woman looks almost like anorexic, then she cannot consider herself as 'beautiful'. On top of that, they advertise all sorts of weight loss schemes, ranging from tablets, magic lotions, all the way to surgical procedures. This is an area where women have wasted so much time and money in their pursuit of the idealized beauty.

What the media does not tell, however, are the numerous underlying consequences, which include the risk of infertility, emotional and psychological scars, illnesses, and in some cases death. Women have been led to believe that unless they are thin as the models that they often see in magazines and beauty pageants for instance, then they are not beautiful enough. Because of this, a lot of eating disorders, concoctions, and *kukukachis* have come about in the pursuit of slimming down.

The enemy does not care about your *weight*; what bothers him most is your capability to bring life to this earth when your body is *healthy*. Sisters, wake up ... You are under attack! The delusion is yet another of Devil's schemes to stop life.

Red Flag #2:
Cost of God's blessings?

Against God's blessing to multiply, the devil is using women to accomplish his goal of stopping life today, just as he had used a woman (Eve) in the Garden of Eden. Now that God's *Word* says multiply, then it means that anything that is opposed to human beings multiplying is definitely not from God but from the devil.

[128]God is the same yesterday, today and forever; and so is His *Word*. That expressly cancels out what people say about the cost of multiplying, claiming that it only applied to the people of early days because life was cheaper then. Such mentality ignores the fact that it is not God who made the cost of living on this earth expensive, but rather our poor decisions. These decisions have on the other hand been as inspired or influenced by the devil so that today we 'cannot afford' to have, say, ten children or more.

---

[128] Hebrews 13: 8; Malachi 3: 6; James 1: 17

Same applies to the numerous of other God's blessings ... they are for free, have no costs attached to them, and are all custom-designed for the wholesome proliferation of life in abundance. We do not earn them, yet we are made worth of them purely through His Love and Grace.

Red Flag #3:
Celebration of same sex relationships

I do not believe that God would say multiply, put seeds in men, and create female bodies that are so equipped for carrying babies amongst the many other things they can do, yet at the same time then create same sex relations. That would imperatively be like calling God 'stupid' because by so doing, He would knowingly be contradicting His own blessing.

In the *Old Testament*, [129]God told Moses to tell His people not to follow the practices of Egyptians where they were coming from, or of the Canaanites where he was taking them to. He told Moses to tell them to only follow His ways. Remember that the Israelites were Gods chosen people who were supposed to worship Him and Him alone. All the other nations worshiped other gods and goddesses, which means they lived sinful lives.

[129] Leviticus 18

Today it means that we as Christians must not live as the people of the world ... sinners ... as Jesus has rescued us from the land of sin ... *our Egypt.* Accordingly, God told Moses a list of sexual practices that the Israelites were not expected to do. He said, for instance:

> *"Thou shalt not lie with mankind, as with womankind: it is abomination."* - Leviticus 18:22 [KJV].

In another version, the same verse reads:

> *"It is disgusting for a man to have sex with another man."* - Leviticus 18:22 [CEV].

Further down there is even a warning:

> *"If a man has sexual relations with another man, they have done a disgusting thing, and both shall be put to death. They are responsible for their own death."* - Leviticus 20:13 [TEV].

Abomination

Today as we see gay / lesbian relationships rise and being celebrated by many, being made to look like it a good thing, we fail to notice the devil as he remains behind the scenes. Fortunately the devil has no new tricks up his sleeve. So he keeps using the same old ones upon every generation, and that makes us more fortunate than the preceding generations because we have the privilege to look back at their lives and learn from how the devil tricked them. That way we may learn as well how we may avoid falling for the same tricks.

As same sex relations is one of the devil's tricks to stop mankind from multiplying, let us then look back at how he used this same trick on our ancestors. Same sex practices are mentioned to have been practiced by those who worshiped gods as it was part of their worship ceremony. Therefore, God told Moses to tell His chosen people not to copy that. In today's terms it would mean that same sex relations are not practiced by those who are followers of Jesus Christ (Christians / the body of Christ / the church). They are rather practiced by those who belong to the world.

Same sex relations are then again mentioned to have been practiced in Sodom and Gomorrah as we read about the men of Sodom who wanted to have sex with Lot's visitors. They were males, who were limited to only recognizing Lot's visitors as just other males and not angels. Lot's response to their request shows us that the practice was bad even then. He (Lot) said to them:

"Friends, I beg you, don't do such a wicked thing!" – Genesis 19: 7 [CEV].

[130]These men were later on struck blind by the angels so that they could not find the door. The following morning they were rained on by burning sulfur and died alongside the entire population that they represented; they attracted God's judgment...!

As children of God we should always seek for guidance in the Bible and not look to the world for answers because we will be deceived if we do. A sizeable portion of the world is following a deceptive leader's guidance – the devil. That is why same sex marriages have been legalized, just like the murdering of innocent babies in abortion rooms has been legalized in the name of human rights. All these are manifestations of the devil's attack on God's blessing and commissioning to multiply.

With all due respect to the freedom of choice, I am not hereby advocating or in support of hating and/or hurting those who practice same sex relationships or abortions. To the contrary, I am trying to rather be supportive to them in affirmatively loving them by way of shining the light of Christ on them, which alone has the power to free everyone from the devil's paws. Take note that condemning them will not help anyone.

---

[130] Genesis 19:11, 23-29

Attack 2: To take away life

Red Flag #1:
[131] *Ancient worship of the god Baal*

As the worship of foreign gods spread all over Israel, the worship of *Baal* was the most popular. It was believed that the god *Baal* had powers to bring rain so that their crops would have a great harvest and they would therefore have plenty of food to eat. A metallic statue would be sculptured to represent the god, which was a half-man-half-bull *thing*. Then its worshipers would have a worship ceremony in front of it. Just like worshippers of God (the true God) would offer sacrifices to Him, so did the worshipers of the god *Baal*.

As for *Baal,* they would bring infants and put them in a burning furnace, which would be next to the statue; thereby offering them as a living sacrifice. What would then follow was that worshipers would then engage in sexual intercourse with each other; bi-sexual, gay and lesbian orgies. For those who would have sex with opposite sex partners, some of the women would conceive. These women would obviously not be able to know for sure who the actual biological father of their child was as they would have had sex with many different men during

---

[131]   Example: 1 Kings 18

such ceremonies.

The babies conceived from those *Baal* worshipping ceremonies would then be born and offered as living sacrifice. This typical group of children were additional to other sacrificial children conceived under normal family settings by the *Baal* worshippers. As the children would burn, the smoke would rise and the worshipers would celebrate.

Barbaric as this practice may sound, you might be surprised to know that similar practices and/or equivalents exist in our society today. Some of you are familiar with 'consulting' ceremonies that purportedly require the use of human reproductive body parts or similar life-pegged organs, with the basic condition that those body parts have to be taken while the coerced donor is still alive. Needless to say, children are the most vulnerable of such malicious practices. Whether a past or current practice, we see in both instances the concerted efforts made by the devil in his hideous mission of taking away life.

Red Flag #2:
Today's worship of the god of Convenience

Relate to how in worship a sacrifice is burnt, and as the smoke rises up to God; it smells sweet and pleasing to Him. The parallel opposite to that is the smoke of dead children; it calls out for judgment like Abel's blood called out on the ground. Taking life away in the form of abortion is one of the "in-thing" these days. It has even gone as far as being legalized in several countries, with children from the age of twelve being allowed to have an abortion free of charge in government hospitals even without parental consent. Some young women have actually adopted it as form of *contraceptive*. Innocent lives are being taken away on a daily basis in abortion clinics, hospitals and even at the back streets by quacks and/or fly-by-night abortionists. It has become a full-fledged industry.

As we claim to be civilized, the devil's influence in our lives turns us into animal-like human beings…plainly barbaric. There is nothing different from the ancient worship of gods and what is happening today. We too are worshiping a god, whom we may simply call *the god of convenience"*. So for convenience sake, babies in the womb are denied the chance to see the light of day simply because they will be an inconvenience to their respective mothers. Some women perceive babies as an inconvenience in the sense that they believe the babies will frustrate their plans; plans to 'enjoy' life *self*-ishly.

The circumstances under which those babies are conceived are irrelevant and thus stand no ground as basis or good reason for an abortion ... and YES, not even rape...! And I do not mention rape here without sensitivity to it; I do know how much anger one can carry for the rapist and anything to do with him, but still that gives no one the right to murder an innocent baby.

I still do not understand how someone or people, in their right mind, can really legalize abortion. Please do not let them fool you with their story of performing it before the baby is formed...'while it's still a foetus...'so they say - there is no such a thing. Believe it or not, life begins at conception. The [132]Bible says that God knew our life before we came to this earth ... Where then does the foetus story fit into this truth?

The moment life begins as a baby is conceived, his or her life is as precious as our life out of our mother's womb. That young life deserves as much protection against harm as ours does. Why is it then, that if someone would kill you by whatever means, the statutory law demands that the person who killed you be put in jail or in some cases be sentenced to death. The law even includes instances where you happen not to be killed but the person as convicted of planning to kill is still found guilty and punishable accordingly. The Law even caters for the

[132] Jeremiah 1: 5-6; Luke 1: 44; Psalms 139: 15-16

condemnation of any accomplice in that context. Yet somehow, the Law then turns a blind eye when it comes to these defenceless young beings.

BEWARE:

It is wrong to take away someone's life,
irrespective of that person's stage of
biological development in life,
be it in or out of the womb.

Abortion is total rebellion against God. Take note that there are no two ways around submission; It is either we rebel or *submit*. It is impossible to do both. It is God's plan for life to continue, for humans to multiply. If we remain submissive to this divine plan, then we will not kill or participate in the killing of babies. But if we choose to rebel, we will go ahead and kill our unborn children. That in itself amounts to being a murder regardless of all the sorts of excuses that the devil might whisper to us.

Like Abel's blood, the blood of all the innocent
babies that we women have murdered cry out to God.

The truth is that what makes a human being human is not the stage of development of his or her body, but the mere existence of his or her spirit. Just like our Father in heaven who created us in His likeness, we too are *spirit beings*. From Creflo

Dollar's teachings, I learnt that I am spirit, who lives in a body and possesses a soul. As such, my body is not me and my soul (which is my mind, will and emotions) is not me either, but only my spirit is me.

Unfortunately the world perceives human beings with reference to their body and soul and by doing so have missed the truth of what a human being really is. The mind and body develop in stages and matures with time, but the spirit is different; it comes from God as mature as it will ever be. This simply means that we come from God, who sends us to this world as a spirit. We come as full-grown, mature human beings. All that happens then from birth to adulthood is merely the growth / development of body and mind in order for the spirit (which is the real being) to be able to fully express him-/her-self through them.

It is common knowledge that a new born baby cannot talk or walk. On a similar note, if God's calling for you is to become a teacher, then that will mean that when He sends you (your spirit) to this earth through your mother's womb, your spirit comes fully aware of its mission. Nevertheless, it has to wait for the mind and body to catch up by way of their maturing with time.

I believe that we are all predestined beings sent by God to each complete our assignment here on earth. That is partly why as we grow up we have certain taste(s) for certain things, yet we cannot explain why. That, in my humble understanding, is the spirit aligning the mind and body to the assignment given by God.

I have never been able to explain why I am so comfortable with staying in doors for days without feeling bored as most people do. I have always had that with me and on many occasions I prefer having the house in total silence. I cherish those quiet moments to just 'being still'. And then I start writing just about anything ... from the end month budget ... to updating my 5 year plan of personal growth. I have been doing this since I was a child and to this day as an adult, writing has been like a norm. During all those phenomenal quiet moments, I have gotten used to my spirit preparing and directing me along my purpose, which she (my spirit) knew about right from the beginning when I entered my mother's womb.

In summary, when abortion is committed, a human being with full potential to accomplish his /her God given mission is murdered. Even though abortion has been legalized, that does not take away the fact that it is murder. It is a lie from the devil that doctors tell women when they often say that before twelve weeks a human being is not a human being but just a blood clot.

Here is an excerpt of an article written by Thomas Horn that I would like to share with you. It depicts God's Love for children, so much that an analogy between religious festivals and a child's biological gestation period can be drawn. You may access the full article via the link provided in the citation at the bottom.

[133]A Gift from God

But the Bible makes it clear that every child is a gift from God. A surprising discovery recently revealed that the Biblical feasts parallel the gestation period of a baby. It seems, once again, the Almighty hid within His *Word* proof of divine inspiration and a token of His love for children.

FEASTS: In Exodus Chapter 12 we find the Passover feast instituted. It was to begin on the fourteenth day of the first month and repeat each year thereafter. During Passover the Jews place an egg, symbolizing new life, on the Passover table.

MEDICAL FACT: On the fourteenth day of the first month the

[133] Thomas Horn. [Online]. *Abortion, Baal Worship, And Breast Cancer.* Available:
         http://www.ovrlnd.com/GeneralInformation/breastcancerandball.html. Accessed: 4 July

mother's egg appears.

FEASTS: The feast of Unleavened Bread must occur the very next night, on the 15th day of the month, or the feast process will fail.

MEDICAL FACT: Fertilization of the egg must occur within 24 hours or the fertilization process will probably fail.

FEASTS: The feast of First fruits occurs next, on the Sunday during the week of Unleavened Bread. It can be from 2-6 days after the feast of Unleavened Bread and is called the Spring Planting of Seed.

MEDICAL FACT: The fertilized egg travels down the tube at its own pace taking anywhere from 2-6 days before it implants. This is the Planting of the Egg.

FEASTS: Pentecost comes 50 days later and, in evangelical circles, celebrates the forming of the Church by the Holy Spirit.
MEDICAL FACT: On the fiftieth day the embryo begins to form into a human foetus.

FEASTS: The Day of Atonement is celebrated on the tenth day

of the seventh month. Blood is taken into the Holy of Holies in the Tabernacle.

MEDICAL FACT: On the tenth day of the seventh month the production of red blood cells is taken over by the bone marrow - the inner sanctum of the baby's tabernacle.

FEASTS: The Feast of Tabernacles follows on the 15th day of the seventh month. Jews celebrate God's breathing the breath of life into Adam.

MEDICAL FACT: By the 15th day of the seventh month the child is capable of breathing air. He or she is a developed "tabernacle" and can be born. However, to achieve maximum strength the child should continue to grow inside its mother for another 80 days. It can thereafter be born and dedicated to the Lord.

FEASTS: 80 days later is the feast of DEDICATION!

Attack 3: **Parenting**

Red Flag #1: 'Liberated' women

Mothers have never been so busy with everything else but to take care of their young ones. Unfortunately the "mummy's job" cannot be delegated to anyone else because the job is only meant for the mom. If anyone else tries to take over for, or from her, the one who ends up suffering most is the child because he/she can feel the difference.

Gone are the days when mothers used to take care of their children and give them all the attention they needed when growing up. Believe you me, it is more than a full time job to raise children; it is a 24 / 7 / 365 job - an all day, every day, all year round job, with no vacation, no sick leave, no option to quit, and definitely no retirement. I am 32 years old now but I still learn a lot from my mother. At a similar level my *Gogo* (Grand*ma*) still dishes out advice to my mother whenever she feels stuck with anything. This is despite the fact that the latter is now 62 years old. Why? - The job continues…!

In the name of liberation, the devil is stealing away the mother's time that ought to be spent with her children. He does this, for instance, by keeping her pre-occupied with work, coming home too tired and too late to even help the kids with their homework or find out how their day was like.

Having children comes with, or requires a lot of selflessness from the mother (and father too). It might even mean forgetting about climbing that "corporate ladder" for a while.

You also cannot afford to have children and still be concerned about natural body changes. Do not you stress about your weight gain, the stretch marks, the cellulite, the different direction that your breast will point at ... it all comes as a package with the new-born.

Red Flag #2: Child negligence

It starts with expectant mothers who drink and smoke all kinds of things that are harmful to the baby, eventually possibly giving birth to underweight children with brain development problems. Take note that the moment of "I'm sorry" is normally way too late to make a difference.

In other cases, children as young as 1 month old are left with nannies or in day-care Centres. These babies do not get to bond with their mothers and/or to feel the warm motherly welcome-to-earth treat. Mostly, they are not breast fed - they are unfairly not given the only proper food that they deserve. This is very harmful to the child's development as breast milk is known to be the best food for the child as it strengthens the immune system and helps in brain development. Despite scientific developments in powder milk formulas, nothing can out-do the mother's breast milk.

When the children are fully grown up enough to eat solid foods, they are fed fast foods and tons of 'junk' because mummy has no time to prepare homemade nutritious meals. Results? Lifestyle diseases like obesity and *Type II* diabetes is no longer a new phenomenon in children; a very serious, yet very common health hazard nowadays.

Mothers have also neglected the nurturing of their children's psychology and have left that job to the likes of TV, video games, PC games, play stations, and the internet. These *hullabies* are left to feed the child's brain with (mostly) 'mental junk'. The kids are also often exposed to visuals that their brains are under-developed to process. They end up believing that what they see on the TV and all the like forms of delusional media they are exposed to are real and/or normal.

That is partly why they are shooting and stabbing each other at school, wrestling, stealing, raping, drinking, smoking, having sex for sport, struggling with being homosexuals, using foul-language, committing suicide, and the list goes on and on. I am inclined to think of children as normally thought of computers, that is, 'Garbage in, Garbage out!'

Guard your gates of receptions, and mind what you feed your own and/or your children's mind with.

All these things could be prevented to a large extent if mothers would dedicate enough time to their children; time to communicate with them, help them with their homework, prepare nutritious meals for them, comfort them, correct them when they go astray, counsel them, set amicable boundaries, pray with them, and just shower them with endless love that only a mother is capable of giving. Most importantly of all is the need to direct them towards appreciating, identifying with, loving and respecting God's *Word*.

Red Flag #3: Setting bad examples for children

From personal experience I can hereby say that being a parent is a wonderful blessing, yet one of the hardest of things one can ever do. With every other thing, you can get away with just *talking-the-talk*, but with parenting you have to also *work-the-work* and that is what makes it harder than most things in life.

A lesson that all of us as parents can learn from raising our children is that children naturally do better in 'Practicals' than in 'Theory'; They may not necessarily do what you tell them to do, but they will most likely follow your footsteps. They tend to watch more than they listen...!

It is very amazing just how we women can be so disrespectful to our husbands and yet expect respect from our children. Strange how parents use obscene language but scold their children for having a *dirty mouth*. Educators know this character-building factor all too well, especially at the lower grades of schooling. Whenever a child is very naughty, uses *strong language*, and/or fights alot with other kids; they immediately know that something is *wrong* in the respective child's homesteads, environment, and/or parents. Therefore if you want to know what is possibly *wrong* with you as a parent, the best mirror is your child(ren).

It is very unfortunate to see just how the devil is using mothers to destroy the future generation. Women are refusing to *submit* to their husbands because they are *liberated* by having an education that *qualifies* them to be able to financially take care of themselves. Then when submission is required of them, they make all sorts of claims and excuses towards filing for a divorce for instance, not realizing that the lesson they are silently teaching their daughters is that with education a woman can play both the father's and mother's role (being both the head and body), which is totally unscriptural. It is like saying that education can *liberate* the *church* to the point where we do not need or can do without Jesus; to take up His role and still be the church, which is impossible.

A woman who marries a man for whom she cares nothing about but only for money is silently teaching her daughter(s) prostitution at its highest level. A woman who lives a faithless life is silently teaching her children that God is not there. A mother who for whatsoever reason(s) then decide to be a lesbian takes away from her sons the privilege of having a male leader in the house to show them how to be a man. Similarly, she takes away from her daughters the privilege of a male to show them what to expect from a husband.

Red Flag #4: Abusing children

Women are often involved, either directly or indirectly, in the abuse of their own and else children. So many children, both female and male alike, have been victims of fathers who sexually abuse them. In so many of these cases, the woman (normally the mother) knows or suspects the occurrence of the malice but does nothing about it. This negligence is sometimes in the name of preventing her marriage from falling apart ... but at whose expense? – the child's! By so doing, such women fail to awaken to the fact that, by the malice happening, it is a clear indication that their marriage has already fallen apart in the first place. Such women are as guilty of abusing their children as the respective transgressing fathers themselves.

Women who themselves verbally abuse their own children by calling them all sorts of negative names and/or words do equally plant negative seeds in their heads. [134]When it comes to correcting the child, something that the Bible encourages parents to, the parents are to do it from a place of love. [135]They are to correct their children when they do wrong in order to teach them that wrong-doing has sour consequences.

For some parents though, they take that a step further and execute it out of anger and not out of love. In extreme cases, some parents do it out of sheer hatred of the particular child or the child's other parent. In most of such situations, the corrective measure actually awakens anger and rebellion instead of repentance in those children's hearts.

I trust that the conscience of a parent will alert him/her whenever he/she is crossing the line in punishing the child. According to child psychologists, a general rule of thumb in this respect is that whatever you do, you should refrain from hitting your child with your bare hands, for example, clapping or boxing them, pushing them around, and the like. Once you use

[134] Proverbs 13: 24; 29:15; Hebrews 12: 5-6
[135] Proverbs 23: 13-14

the hands or part of your body, it becomes man-handling, not corrective action any more ... and that potentially falls under children abuse.

Attack 4: **Yearning for Control**

Most women are under what I prefer to call the 'control-freak-syndrome'. It stems from what I decode to be of a good nature as we yearn to be in control of just about everything pertaining to our lives and the immediate surroundings. Come to think of it - we often try by all means to be controlling of our children and husbands, our friends and even (for those who can afford...) exercise control over personal-care service-providers such as hair-dressers, beauty-therapists, and waiters/waitresses.

This manner of tendency extends to care-givers, people at whose mercy we often find ourselves, for instance the nurses. I can imagine a bed-ridden *control-freak-patient* with medical machines attached; the beeping-sounds and graphs becoming alarming as they get frustrated trying to control what the nurse(s) must or must not do...! The syndrome is more prevalent in women and silently manifests in the way we relate with our husbands, children, and surroundings.

How

Quite often, we choose not to listen to our children. Instead, we often prefer to force our ideologies of life onto them or unconsciously strive to live our unachieved dreams through them. On the other side of the coin, we obviously have the responsibility to guide them. Nevertheless, there is a very thin line between guiding and leading a child one hand, versus dictating to- and frog-matching them along a certain way or path of life. At any point in time, these two approaches are mutually exclusive.

Despite both approaches being claimed to be founded on love for the child, the latter approach unfortunately seems to take-over almost naturally in most of us. It is for that reason that the former approach always calls for a continuous conscious awareness of one's *selfish* or *egocentric* inclinations. Only then will the choice between the two approaches yield the right results for the child.

In the unfortunate instances where dictatorship to children or anyone else prevails, there is one most common kind of out-come, i.e. rebellion. In the best case scenarios, it provokes apathy, receives false respect and faked humility in those who are victims thereof. In most cases, these victims happen to be our own husbands, children or the closest of family members by default-setting because of the typically enormous amount of time shared together on a regular basis.

On a lighter note, at-least the *victims* get to receive first hand a taste of dictatorship from us, Ha! The styles and extents are way too diverse to debate in this book and are hereby not explored. However, the poignant question is: WHERE DOES ALL THIS FORCEFUL LEADERSHIP COME FROM?

Well, from my personal observation, hear me well at this point and with no judgment. I do not mean to come off like I have much of a background in the study of human psychology, but I do discern that most of the extreme instances of *control-freak-behaviour* can be traced back to past experiences whereby the contextual women have been victims of abuse themselves, especially sexual abuse.

Take for instance a young female who get to be man-handled and/or sexually abused by a man she trusts, be it her father, uncle, cousin, brother, priest, preacher, friend, teacher or any male figure that she is under normal circumstances supposed to trust. That young girl goes through an instantaneous moment of *loss of control* during such a bout of attack. I do believe that such an experience does more damage psychologically than it does physically. One of the immediate effects of such an ordeal is the development of a very pronounced defence mechanism … being on full guard against her surroundings, especially around the male species.

The defence mechanism is understandably installed and activated whenever the girl is around the one(s) who directly hurt her. Unfortunately, the mind subconsciously (and generously) extends the activation to include those who did not directly hurt her but are in some way look-alikes to the perpetrator(s). In most cases, these look-alikes are not out to get her but rather have the interest to do exactly the opposite, which is love and protect her.

Before we progress any further with this, I would like you to for a moment focus on you rather than take the position of seeing this character girl as a distant being or victim. A good bunch of women have had a share of such un-dear circumstances to varying degrees, with some having experienced worse scenarios than others. My point is this – at one point in life you probably faced a situation that put you in a position of exercising ZERO control over it and now as an adult or young adult you are still fighting back to regain your control over that situation.

As you reflect on your particular past ordeal, I wish you could ask yourself the question, 'Do I always get the ultimate target results, emotionally and in a tangible sense?' The answer to that question varies depending on what you often seek to control, i.e. *people* versus *things* around you. Sometimes the *control-freak-tendencies* are manifested with both *people* and *things* as the subjects. Debatable as the question may be, I guess the answer in more than 50% of the instances is a big NO especially whenever the subject is a person(s). This is partly because you are simply fighting an old battle that has just been masked as a new one.

In response to the masked 'new' versions of your old battle, your feedback may take one or more forms of consistent default reaction(s). This reaction(s) is almost like a reflex action … it gets to be engaged with little or no conscious choice regardless of the situation at hand. In often cases the scenario is almost always misinterpreted by virtue of one's bias as a result of being subconsciously on guard.

There are also passive forms of default reactions. These include, for instance, an extreme demand for perfection from children or subordinates, sensitivity towards disorder even in the slightest of forms, obsession with particular activities such as cleaning, unravelled feathers as a result of otherwise noble statements coming from a particular gender or category of people, and so on. At a closer look, these default reactions are simply the result of having been trapped inside a past experience and reliving it over and over again with different people and/or situations.

Towards dealing with the *control-freak-tendencies*, it is important to awaken to, and appreciate the fact that you are no longer in that same old situation. Fighting back by exercising a controlling arm especially on the people around you is simply like punching in the air ... it will get you exhausted, often leave you drained, and without the intended results.

Until the actual past experience is consciously apprehended, it may be very difficult to redress it. A psychologist may help or a concerted retrospection aimed at setting-free the offender and yourself. It may be a very torturous experience but I have learnt one important thread that holds everything together: LOVE conquers ALL. To drive this point home, I hereby wish to share with you my intimate personal experience.

My Personal account

Difficult as it may be for me to absorb this fact, the painful truth is that my father started abusing me sexually at a very tender age. This is an experience that I wish no child should ever be subjected to. I chose to internally suppress the bitter feelings about it while externally trying to move on as though it never happen. Over the years as I grew up to a young adult, I grew deeper and deeper into an abyss of mixed feelings and thoughts about the painful experience. The inherent anger, self-blaming, the WHY?, the WHEN will he apologize?, the WHAT if?, the HOW can I revenge?, the suicidal thoughts and attempts … It was all a live-nightmare. Somehow, I almost perfected the art of bottling in and/or masking my hurtful feelings.

To add salt into injury, or perhaps as a way of creating a proactive self-defence virtual wall, my father made the environment at home to be very fearful. He was extremely physically abusive to us; my elder sister and my mother. He was really a natural at that. Needless to say, I grew up constantly wishing to escape from the life that I had, living in a home where fear of my father ruled. I always wished that he was different, wishing that he could change to become a loving and caring dad. I longed and hoped that he could change to someone that I could run to for protection instead of the figure I wanted to run away from as a source of danger.

Now because I was young, I had no choice but to grow up in

my household and take whatsoever came with that. In short, I had no control over the situation at home. But at some stage I summoned enough courage to make my mother aware of what was happening to me. Being a nurturing mother as always, and for which I am forever grateful, she since then made sure that my father was nowhere near us. She instituted a legal separation from him.

At this point it might sound like I'm condoning breaking-up of married couples and you may be thinking, hey, what became of the message: '*submit* to your husband no matter what happens'? No-o-o-o! - it is not even close. My mother exercised submission throughout her 22 years of live-in marriage. It was not until when she got to know that my father was harming me that she chose to separate from him as a desperate measure of protecting us as her children. In fact, she refused to legally divorce him at the request of her legal counsel and still *submits* to him from a safe distance / space. She has always prayed for him because she believes that marriage is a one way ticket to a new divine level of being.

To cut a long story short, as an adult I have occasionally been with my father and after a long struggle with forgiveness, I was finally able to forgive him and let go of the pain and anger that came as a result of his actions. I have prayed for him and put back-together most, if not all, of the broken pieces of my love for him as a father. Today I'm honoured and proudly happy to update you with the news that he recently got born again. Over the last approximately 3 years, he has also been freed from alcohol abuse, which I guess significantly contributed to his abusive and destructive behaviour.

As a result of my childhood experience, I unconsciously grew up into a *control-freak*, a behaviour that I consider to be a very troubling spirit for anyone to have. I developed an obsessive behaviour over certain things. At the top of the list was cleanliness. As you can readily concur with me, it is a good thing to be clean and live in a clean house or environment. However, it is another thing to be obsessed about it.

I somehow strived to regain some kind of control in my life, which came in the form of controlling my immediate surroundings by making sure that everything is neat and tidy at all times. At first it seemed like a good quality to have as it even got me an award of neatness in high school, but over the years it proved to be a burden. I developed a way in which I prefer my clothes to be folded, shoes arranged, order in the kitchen, how the bed must be made, and so on. And may I add that raising young children and at the same time expecting a spotless house 24/7 is a sure set-up for stress … believe you me I have really had the blunt end of making it all gel-up.

Through my walk in faith in God, I have learnt to let go of all this unhealthy obsessive behaviour. This is more especially because I realized that I was creating the same type of fearful environment in my home … the same kind of environment that my father had created when I was young. I awaked to that awareness when I took account of my children's behaviour.

Whenever I would enter the house from a long day at work, my children would welcome me with hugs and kisses. Immediately after receiving that warmth, I would return it with a session of finding and expressing faults in them for not maintaining cleanliness in the house. Slowly the hugs and kisses were replaced by apt reports on who did or did not do what … blaming each other for either this or that and naively bullying each other, be it literary or through manipulation.

All the militant effort to control neatness in my house has had very little or nothing to do with me being a cleanliness-conscious person. A careful retrospection awoke me to the understanding that all I had been fighting for was control, the very control that I lost or never got a chance to exercise when

I most needed to as a young child. That understanding was as far as my brain capacity would take me. It took God's grace to actually awaken to the fact that I never really had any control at any point in time anyway. No one does ... except the Almighty Living God, who is in perfect control of the entire universe.

At work as a beauty therapist, I see it all the time; people, especially women will go as far as priding themselves on how fussy they are about the treatment that they book for. Many times before starting a treatment we have had some clients expressly say "I'm very fussy; please make sure you do a perfect job". I always book myself with such characters because I know that most of the time all they need is love and care, someone to talk to, to feel safe. My edge is in that I can identify with where their demands are coming from and can relate with their battle.

It should be made expressly clear here that it does not mean that you were necessarily sexually abused if you are a control freak. Sexual abuse is just one of the afflictions in a million of possible causes. The *control-freak-behaviour* stems from going through any situation that corners one to a position of temporally loss of control or helplessness. As a result, one then develops a defence mechanism of safe-guarding 'their' control.

Conclusion

*W*e have learned different lessons from the selected women's lives. All the lessons have had to do with them either *submitting* or not *submitting* to God's *Word*, or God's-ordained authority. We have seen that the things we go through today are no different from what they went through them days. That justifiably makes them fit to be our *teachers*.

Most importantly, I hope that the greatest lesson that you have learnt is that we cannot *submit* to God - who in turn requires us to *submit* to the authority ordained by Him and placed in our lives - if we are not His children. Therefore the first step to submission is accepting Jesus Christ who, through His *grace*, will then teach us how to *submit* and grant us the strength and wisdom required to do so.

My humble request to all women is to always remember that we have a great job and responsibility bestowed upon us: (i) as helpers of our husbands, (ii) as pillars of strength and support to them, (iii) as the body of our marriage, and (iv) as the ones whom God entrusted to carry and nurse His precious souls when they arrive on earth.

I hope and pray that we may all awaken to the realization of just how valuable and divine our Job is. In that realization, I hope that we may stop trying to do *men's jobs* and stop trying to change our husbands, but rather to pray to our Lord Jesus to help us perform our duties as best as we have divinely been equipped to.

As we soldier on, let us be well prepared to overcome the devil and his uncanny ways. Let us wear the *Whole Armour of God* well, putting all our trust in God, and submissively exercising faith in God's grace as we seek to become living testimonies in our respective families and society.

May God ALWAYS be with you in your particular, very specially and custom-designed journey of submission as a woman led by the Holy Spirit. We are ALL *Work-In-Progress*. Be blessed...!!!

The Whole Armour of God

[10]*Finally, build up your strength in union with the Lord and by means of his mighty power.* [11]*Put on all the armour that God gives you, so that you will be able to stand up against the Devil's evil tricks.* [12]*For we are not fighting against human beings but against the wicked spiritual forces in the heavenly world, the rulers, authorities, and cosmic powers of this Dark Age.* [13]*So put on God's armour now! Then when the evil day comes, you will be able to resist the enemy's attacks; and after fighting to the end, you will still hold your ground.* [14]*So stand ready, with truth as a belt tight around your waist, with righteousness as your breastplate,* [15]*and as your shoes the readiness to announce the Good News of peace.* [16]*At all times carry faith as a shield; for with it you will be able to put out all the burning arrows shot by the Evil One.* [17]*And accept salvation as a helmet, and the word of God as the sword which the Spirit gives you.* 18Do all this in prayer, asking for God's help. Pray on every occasion, as the Spirit leads.*

Ephesians 6: 10 – 18 [TEV]

THE END

www.ingramcontent.com/pod-product-compliance
Lightning Source LLC
LaVergne TN
LVHW041151080426
835511LV00006B/549